The Past in Contemporary Society: Then, Now

The past is a whole range of different 'heritages' which now influence contemporary life to a quite extraordinary degree. *The Past in Contemporary Society: Then, Now* is an innovative book which discusses this phenomenon as 'current affairs' and forecasts the future of the past in the 1990s.

The author examines contemporary relationships between past and present, bringing out their complexity and ambivalence. He analyses uses of 'pastness' to meet current needs at personal, national and international levels, ranging from 'heritage' activities such as scholarly research and museum curation, through conservation practices, to media coverage, leisure, tourism and commercial advertising. One theme to emerge is 'Heritage' as commodity, a device at one level for personal choice and at another for selling anything from computers to fantasy.

The book provides prescriptions for responsible management, development and thoughtful interpretation. Devised in part to explain something of what lies behind the heritage industry to its many consumers, such as visitors to sites and museums, and writers and readers of tourist leaflets, this appositely illustrated volume will be essential reading for all those involved professionally with the contemporary past, be it as custodians, managers, interpreters or exploiters. It will be particularly useful to the growing number of 'heritage' students and their teachers.

Peter J. Fowler is Professor of Archaeology at the University of Newcastle upon Tyne.

THE HERITAGE
CARE
PRESERVATION
MANAGEMENT

Editor in chief   Andrew Wheatcroft

The Heritage: Care–Preservation–Management programme has been designed to serve the needs of the museum and heritage community worldwide. It publishes books and information services for professional museum and heritage workers, and for all the organisations that service the museum community.

The programme has been devised with the advice and assistance of the leading institutions in the museum, and heritage community, at an international level, with ICOM and ICOMOS, with the national and local museum organisations and with individual specialists drawn from every continent.

Museums Without Barriers: *A new deal for disabled people*
Fondation de France and ICOM

Museums and the Shaping of Knowledge
Eilean Hooper-Greenhill

Forward Planning: *A handbook of business, corporate and development planning for museums and galleries*
Edited by Timothy Ambrose and Sue Runyard

Museums 2000: *Politics, people, professionals and profit*
Edited by Patrick Boylan

The Industrial Heritage: *Managing resources and uses*
Judith Alfrey and Tim Putnam

The Past in Contemporary Society

Then, Now

Peter J. Fowler

London and New York

First published 1992
by Routledge
11 New Fetter Lane, London EC4P 4EE

Simultaneously published in the USA and Canada
by Routledge
a division of Routledge, Chapman and Hall, Inc.
29 West 35th Street, New York, NY 10001

Printed in Great Britain by
Butler & Tanner Ltd, Frome and London

British Library Cataloguing in Publication Data available from the British Library

Library of Congress Cataloging in Publication Data available upon request

ISBN 0 415 06726 X
    0 415 07130 5 (pbk)

Printed on permanent paper in accordance with American NISO Standards.

to Cilla
who always said
'Now then'

'I love history – so old'

Michael Caine in Alan Alda's *Sweet Liberty* (1986)

Contents

Contents

Illustrations

Illustrations

Acknowledgements

No one is responsible for this essay other than the author but a host of people, usually unknowingly, have contributed to it by providing background and stimulation, mainly by talking to him and letting him watch or join in their activities. In that sense, I am happy to acknowledge a general contribution over the years from colleagues, especially in the Council for British Archaeology, the Forestry Commission, the National Trust and the Royal Commission on the Historical Monuments of England. While they may not thank me for incriminating them, I hope they will not mind my saying so.

More immediately, occasions with and the writings of Christopher Chippindale, Henry Cleere, Hester Davis, Robert Hewison, David Lowenthal, Bob McGimsey, Roger Mercer, Kevin Robins, Charles Thomas, Peter Ucko, Sue Wilkinson and my students have left their imprint, though all are probably unaware of this. My three daughters, Rachel, Ruth and Brigid, have sensitised me, but again without realising it, to relevant current affairs in, respectively, leisure and recreation management, arts administration and politics, and Melanie Whewell has helped alert me to issues on the local government scene.

During 1989–90 I was fortunate enough to be a participant in 'Heritage Workshop', an informal and continuing series of occasions run jointly by the Centre for Urban and Regional Studies and the Department of Archaeology, both University of Newcastle upon Tyne. To it come many of those involved in heritage matters throughout the north of England. I would also gladly acknowledge the serendipitous but significant visual and philosophical stimulation afforded, I suspect partly unintentionally, by the images provided on my doorstep by the National Garden Festival, Gateshead. Over many visits during the summer and autumn of 1990, I established a vibrant love–hate relationship with its many 'heritage-on-the-hoof' scenarios.

Acknowledgements

I learnt much, too, during my travels for another book with Mick Sharp, and am extremely grateful to him for providing a sample of his photographic work to grace these pages. Indeed, in one sense the realisation of this book, and specifically Chapter 6 in it, derives from our discussions and the far too ambitious first draft of the consequentially miniaturised Chapter 3 in our joint *Images of Prehistory* (CUP, 1990).

Chapters 1 and 2 here derive from my inaugural lecture at the University of Newcastle upon Tyne and I acknowledge the presence and ambivalent remarks of my Vice-Chancellor on that occasion. Two successive Deans of Arts, Richard Bailey and Jerry Paterson, have signally encouraged my 'heritage' interests, the latter going far beyond the bounds of decanal duty by volunteering to read a penultimate typescript. My greatest debt is nevertheless to Priscilla Boniface who taught me how to use a word-processor and thereafter ensured that I sat down and used it. Somehow the machine has incorporated not a few of her ideas too ...

All the photographs are by the author except for thirteen by Mick Sharp (Pls 6, 10, 20, 21, 22, 23, 25, 26, 27, 28, 29, 38 and 46), one (Pl. 1) from the National Monuments Record (Crown Copyright reserved), one by Chris Chippindale (Pl. 44) and one (Pl. 32) by an unknown photographer.

Finally, I thank Elizabeth Fowler for constructing the index.

Abbreviations

Newspapers and magazines

BAN	*British Archaeological News* (CBA)
DM	*The Daily Mail*
DT	*The Daily Telegraph*
EC	*The Evening Chronicle* (Newcastle upon Tyne)
ES	*The Evening Standard* (London)
G	*The Guardian*
I	*The Independent*
J	*The Journal* (Newcastle upon Tyne)
LN	*Leisure News*
Mag	*Magazine* (as of O, ST, EH and NT: see below)
O	*The Observer*
ST	*The Sunday Times*
T	*The Times*

Others

BBC	British Broadcasting Corporation
CBA	Council for British Archaeology
EH	English Heritage (The Historic Buildings and Monuments Commission for England)
NT	The National Trust for England, Wales and Northern Ireland
RCHME	Royal Commission on the Historical Monuments of England

Author's note

In the many cases where a quotation is not specifically referred to one of the above newspapers or other bibliographical source, it comes from an information leaflet, tourist brochure or other printed ephemera about the site/area being discussed. With a few exceptions as indicated, all were available in 1990.

Throughout, the date of all calendrical references is 1990 unless otherwise indicated. This applies specifically to references to the media and to the illustrations where usually only a month is quoted.

Preface

'Then, Now' was the title of my inaugural lecture on 20 January 1986, at the University of Newcastle upon Tyne, following my appointment to the Chair of Archaeology there in October 1985. My application, written in April 1985, referred to the then present as 'the age of the "heritage industry"'. I doubt if anyone noticed but that must have been one of the first uses of the phrase 'the heritage industry'.

That 'age' persists, though taking on new shapes and meaning in the five subsequent years which have now produced a post-Thatcher phase in a puzzled, post-modernist society. Here, I set out to explore in the context of that society now what words like 'heritage' and 'past' actually mean in practice, at unique personal levels and, if such be the case, at national level. This is a topic I have been pursuing for thirty years and more, initially as a side-line in the professional life of an archaeologist and teacher. Subsequently it became more central in the 1970s when, with my increasing involvement in 'public archaeology', it became apparent that, not least with an international dimension, there was both academic point and social relevance to my curiosity about the ambivalences in the relationship between past and present.

That phase was marked in book form by Chapters 1 and 6 of my *Approaches to Archaeology* (1977). Subsequently, six years (1979–85) as head of a national heritage agency were years during which I came to think of an august body in precisely those terms while simultaneously 'heritage' itself came to be an ambiguous and emotive word. The next five years trying, among other things, to rationalise the field to teach a self-imposed course grandly called 'Heritage, Management and Society', are among the immediate stimulants to this essay.

In it, I am most obviously concerned with a British, more accurately I guess an English, perspective. Constrained geographically and culturally in my viewpoint, I am even more conscious of a temporal limitation.

Preface

During the writing, the past, not in the past tense but as a very contemporary phenomenon daily manifesting itself in interactions with society here and not in a foreign country, simply took over the book. Curiously, this experience paralleled, but in reverse, that of Robert Hewison who, in setting out to write what eventually came to be *Future Tense: A New Art for the Nineties* (1990), found that 'the past took over' and resulted in *The Heritage Industry* (1987).

This view of 'then', then, can be ascribed with precision to the six months from 1 July to 31 December 1990. Not only was the book written then, in fact in July, August and December, either side of the University autumn term, but the majority of my photographs and the great bulk of the exemplary material belong specifically to that period. It was not what I intended, for I had assiduously assembled as my potential sources an archive of relevant documentation from the 1970s and 1980s; but would I now have it otherwise? My analogue is the theatre or art critic, writing of the contemporary stage or art exhibitions, just as my subject is the contemporaneous past and my theme its dynamic with present-day people as 'current affairs'; especially as witnessed during the latter half of 1990.

In addition to the constraints of place, culture and time, of course my view is subjective. Much of that which stimulated it comes directly from what I have seen and heard, whom I have talked and listened to, above all perhaps from what I have read – and indeed was still reading as I wrote. My debt to the daily and periodical press is enormous: it, and certain writers especially, have provided, often unwittingly, a never-failing quarry. Because so much of relevance and stimulation dropped on to my plate from the world of the printed and broadcast media between July and December 1990, I have not had to search either very hard or systematically.

This is then no scientific analysis or deeply learned discourse. It is a sort of commentary, one side of a chat about ourselves, our attitudes to the past and the, to me, quite staggeringly large influence that a whole range of different pasts have on the present. Many aspects are but touched on, for example fiction, music, architecture, travel; some, such as science, the law, film and drama, are not even mentioned, for the field is vast once you stop to think about it. Many specialists will doubtless find my mention of their areas of interest unsatisfactory but I have deliberately gone for variety rather than completeness, intending the material to be taken as exemplary and indicative rather than definitive. Even so, the coverage is highly selective and the omissions will probably offend too. Nevertheless, my hope is to have provided an introduction for the doubtless mythical 'general reader' to a highly complex, and in my view significant, relationship of apparently disparate activities at a moment in time. The eclecticism of my treatment as well as of my selections, and the implication overall that all is metaphor, accord with the nature of the very phenomenon here discussed.

Many others have, as I realise only too well, discussed the issues here with greater learning and wisdom than I have brought to bear, but I doubt if anyone before this moment can have been subject to quite so much 'pastness' as there is around now *and be so aware of it*. The Bibliography attempts to provide entries to a whole series of overlapping fields of enquiry germane to the discussion.

The mere passage of time of course produces more and more 'history'; we are creating, even inventing lots of it too. Much more of this larger quantity is being made available than ever and, most significantly, an increasingly greater effort seems to be going into either promoting past-ness or promoting something else by using it. Any excuse I have for this essay can only be in its immediacy, in its attempt to pin down if only for momentary and superficial examination what we are doing, cumulatively and collectively, to the past, what it is doing to us, and some of the consequences which arise from these very lively and ambivalent inter-actions at the start of the last decade of the twentieth century.

The above, fairly obviously, was meant to be the last paragraph of the Preface but, characteristically pat on cue as I have now come to expect in writing of the past in the present, irresistible words appositely make themselves available literally at this moment in time. They happen to be those of the Archbishop of Canterbury, himself a great friend to archaeology, and they come in his last New Year's Day message today, subsuming in three sentences what has taken me (minus the theocentric assumption) twelve chapters to try to express:

> I do ... see some justification for calling it the 'Now' generation. The past is more than snapshot nostalgia. Without a deeper sense of the past we may lose gifts God has given us for handling the present.

University of Newcastle upon Tyne
1 January 1991

Past introductions

In the beginning ...   1

In the beginning was the past, and the past was with whoever happened to be living at the time.

Such an obvious crib is taken, without sacrilegious intent, from a very old and well-known collection of history, myth and legend, still the world's best-selling book. Its second part tells of events some two thousand years ago. They involved the Romans, then at the start of their many appearances in countless heritage productions, and an authentically historic hero-figure of traditional form who may or may not, depending on your point of view, have been the Son of God. The first part deals with earlier times, much of which is now called 'prehistory' by archaeologists (though not by many others).

The whole is, of course, primarily of religious significance, both for Christians and for students of the history of religion whether or not they are Christian. The Bible is also a primary source of evidence for archaeological and historical studies irrespective of its religious nature; and those studies themselves are constantly examined by Christians and those of various religious persuasions for any light such academic research may throw on theology and what people want to believe. Studiously ignoring such issues, through the winter of 1990–1 a remarkably conventional exhibition called 'The Bible and Archaeology' ran uncontroversially at the British Museum.

The generalities behind the particulars of the previous two paragraphs are the meat of this book. Its agenda, sometimes overt, sometimes implicit, concerns scholarship and bias, methodology and interpretation, beliefs and irreverence, seriousness and fun, history and hype, altruism and greed, dismay and display, and, above all and throughout, the interplay in a complex of ambivalence of us and our pasts, the past and us late in 1990 (Pl. 1).

From our point of view now, to observe that 'In the beginning was the past' is more or less true; strictly speaking the past began a micro-second after the beginning of time. But, of course, just as Adam and Eve could have started debating the nature of their past in second two, by second five they would have been arguing about different interpretations of their joint and several pasts. Similarly, but more to the point, our contemporary views of 'then' are as new as today. Meanwhile, what once was, both generally and predictably, affects our life across a range from the trivial to the fundamental. Replacing an 'old age' with a new is as much about rethinking attitudes to pasts as starting new activities with a view to a future time.

The current shaping of such rethinking, like the past itself, is very much with us. Various versions of contemporary relationships with what has been, and very much is, have been expressed in books which have subsequently become landmarks in the development of a late-twentieth-century perception of its pasts. David Lowenthal's *The Past is a Foreign Country* (1985) provided the solid academic foundation and much food for cerebration. Patrick Wright's *On Living in an Old Country* (1986) gave the thinking man's reaction on returning in the mid-1980s to a country apparently obsessed with its past, and Robert Hewison interpreted the phenomenon in cultural and political terms in *The Heritage Industry* (1987).

My curiosity here is, at one level, about the uses we make of the past; but, at another, it moves into that ill-defined territory in which we do things for, and to, a whole range of pasts. What do we expect of them? Are *communal* attitudes of mind suggested by such actions and aspirations? And if we are forced to move towards the fringes of what are really contemporary questions for the psychologist, what about the minds of our prehistoric predecessors? It is surely significant in itself that precisely one of archaeologists' contemporary concerns is 'cognitive archaeology', that is an attempt to probe the possibilities of understanding not just what people did, not even why they did it, but rather what they themselves thought were their reasons for doing something. We want to discover something of our predecessors' minds.

That is ambitious, for it is difficult enough to establish simply what happened for long periods in the past, never mind gain agreement on sequence, chronology and significance. The reason for this is a truism: the past is not an immutable, monolithic slab of time just waiting to be 'revealed' or, in archaeology's case, lying there ready to be 'discovered'. Nor does it contain a rigid framework of events 'meaning' only one thing. Interpretation changes with time, as indeed historiography and archaeology's own history witness. Discovery and research reflect as well as promote changes in the past as perceived, in attitudes to a series of changing pasts. 'Then', although it has happened, and cannot change itself, far from being dead is dynamic, for essentially it is a construct of our minds. In a very real sense it is *our* past (wherever we may be born or live), for, to a degree, we fashion it as we will rather than just accepting it as it is, never mind as it was.

This interactive process goes further. It is not simply a matter of how we shape the past but what the past does to us, both individually and communally. A person may derive his or her deepest satisfaction in life by building up a collection of particular old artefacts; a society may evolve a vernacular architectural tradition and then somehow create the circumstances in which that tradition is raided to produce lifeless pastiche in contemporary buildings which its members then have to contemplate (Pl. 2). Indeed, we shape elements of our present in the light of those parts of the past we select for imitation and emulation. The cultivation of 'Victorian values' in Thatcher's Britain, for example, was a conscious selection of bits of a past for political motives, a move which unconsciously reminded us that the Victorians themselves harked back to the supposed chivalrous ideals of romantic medieval times. Yet, as each generation finds, when we arrive there, when we have rediscovered and revamped a past, it is never what it was or even what we thought it was going to be. Our mere intervention transmutes it.

As a society, for example, we spend millions of pounds on dilapidated old buildings and special street furniture to preserve the centre of an historic town, a process parodied as 'ye olde-ing'; we are then proud of, or disappointed by, the resultant 'oldified', *de luxe* and Duluxed middle-class ghetto where architect speaks unto doctor and both send Christmas cards to the Chief Planning Officer. Such a visual transformation may be justified politically, socially, economically, but do not let us deceive ourselves that we have done anything other than create a 'now', not re-create a 'then'.

Archaeologically speaking, of course, such a process is fine. We have merely added another layer to the fabric of the town with visible, material effect, just like medieval burgher, eighteenth-century gentleman and nineteenth-century businessman. In time, our own 'conservation' impact will be recorded, studied, interpreted and doubtless preserved for its own historic interest, representative of its age. Indeed, so great has been the visual impact of such schemes that the later twentieth century has already selectively left its mark on the urban fabric almost as much in conservation terms as in the commercial redevelopments widely regarded as its more characteristic trait.

It is because there is now so much activity and not inconsiderable financial expenditure in relation to actual and imagined 'thens' that some people have begun to wonder where all this worthy effort is taking us (Pl. 3). As conservation and heritage promotion have gained their own momentum, it seems worthwhile to pause to think about not just the selectivity of the process itself but also its effects on our own group psychology. Should we not ponder, for example, the degree to which people help create, participate in and reflect a perception of some sort of common past? It is probably more correct to see them dipping into a selection of items from a common menu of episodic pasts, themselves selectively retained.

A facet of my theme is that for many people the past, or a disconnected string of episodic pasts, concerns a vague 'then', a 'time before' in Eliot's phrase. It is often embodied in artefacts ranging, for both cultural and highly personal reasons, from matchboxes to Mycenae, from a seaside souvenir to a Monet. Such 'thens' do not involve a sense of a sequential, correlated past. They are not about history in the sense of either a rational investigation of time past or the coherent result, narrative or otherwise, of such enquiry. A salient characteristic of this sort of 'then' is its selectivity for preconceived visions of some parts of some of our yesterdays (Pl. 4).

Tourism is a great promoter and user of such eclecticism. By the mid-1980s tourism was already Britain's second biggest earner of foreign currency. Nearly 200 million site visits were made in 1984; by 1989, of some 330 million visits altogether, over 200,000 were to each of at least 54 historic properties. 3.25 million visits were made to Westminster Abbey, 2.7 million to the Tower of London and Tower Bridge combined (Pl. 5). Spending by visitors to historic properties in England in 1989 was about £137 million, revenue having risen over ten years by 59 per cent (*English Heritage Monitor 1990* provides such figures throughout).

About 40 per cent of foreign tourists in 1989, a higher proportion than for any other activity, gave visiting historic sites and cities or towns as a particularly important reason in their decision to visit Britain. A powerful attraction is the combination of visible history *and* beautiful countryside. Though visitor-numbers are growing at real industrial plants and factories such as Sellafield and Pilkington's glassworks, another attraction is the country's redundant industrial power base. It can be made appealing as well as interesting, as at Ironbridge, Beamish and elsewhere, when its redundancy has been cleaned up and interpreted for them, even to the extent of being improved by authentic but non-original additions.

Tourists come for those, and because our fields are green, are surrounded by hedges and walls, and are pricked with farms and woods in a visual patchwork of colourful variety changing with region and season. The past-time dimension, however, hardly comes into popular appreciation of the landscape, nor in a sense does it need to. Yet the interest of the landscape is so much greater, for the British landscape is almost entirely man-made or at least man-influenced (Pl. 6). The whole island is for practical purposes a single archaeological site rather than a tract of land containing hundreds of thousands of sites. What irony, therefore, that much of the conservation protection it enjoys is for its 'natural' beauty.

At a time when the driving force of the conservation movement is a concern for environmental quality, at best expressed as ecological soundness, at worst green emotiveness, typically of the heritage scene it is paradoxical to have to assert the historical, anthropogenic constituent of the countryside. Especially is this so as it is anthropoid we, not Nature, who have made such a mess of it over the last three decades. It is a sign of the times that wryness, perhaps even guilt, about our abuse of our environment leads to attempted humour, often a sensitive indicator of stress. History and archaeology have for long provided cartoonists' material, though often of a clichéd variety. Now, familiar situations are given a green twist. Cavemen, for example, can be shown in earnest discussion about not hunting dinosaurs to extinction; Stonehenge can be envisaged as the structural remains of an incomplete motorway interchange aborted in the face of environmental pressure groups.

Whenever and for whatever reasons we decide to take action in relation to an historic structure or landscape, all that we are actually doing, if we think of our act as part of a process expressed as a graph, is intervening at a point on its curve of decay. Such intervention may, at one extreme, convert the curve into a vertical line if we destroy the site; at the other, it may break the curve by diverting it into a less steep downward incline. At best we can but slow down decay. It therefore becomes important to recognise where in the life-span of the structure, where on its curve of decay, our intervention is occurring. Understanding of this radically affects not only what we can do but what we should and should not do. The latter point itself questions our objectives, and probably our motives, in intervening in the first place.

Implicit in much of this is the concept of planning the past; its executives are 'heritage managers', some of them consciously so (Chapter 7). Such phrases betoken a change, a conscious change, in our relationships to the past and its physical presence today. Of course people have previously shaped their own pasts. Medieval monks, for example, were notoriously good at it, to the benefit of their House on earth rather than their anticipated domicile elsewhere; Shakespeare was doing it much of his time, and the results of his 'shaping' of English history strongly influence present perceptions of it. Now, by promoting the concept and practice of management in our dealing with the structurally surviving past, we are openly saying that we can not only fix it but also manipulate it. Are we not in fact doing just that, unconsciously and at times perhaps with forethought? This is rather different from just simply preserving it, conserving it, restoring it, re-creating it.

Preservation to re-creation

2

Preservation is where many of us came in. We believed that essentially, in the face of threat, to keep something of historic value was better than losing it. At least that kept the options open, options lost for ever once the value had been destroyed. Much preservation activity, however, initially gave little constructive thought to the future of that which might be saved. Typical reactions were 'Let's rescue it and give it to a museum' or 'Let's save it by giving it to the National Trust'. Pity, as we can now see, those institutions accepting such altruistic gifts without a great deal of thought about what was to be done with the preserved history or the on-costs of perpetual curatorship.

Still today, few people have much idea of the price of preservation alone, never mind the costs of conservation, interpretation and promotion. The past does not come cheap. That we can easily be talking of millions of pounds just to stop the loss has been well publicised in the 1980s, notably by the 'saving' of major country houses and works of art. Between £1 million and £5 million is typically the cost of acquiring a major house like Kedleston and Calke Abbey or other property for the public; and merely consolidating a major monument, thereby extending its life as a ruin in good repair for some twenty-five years, can easily cost the same again. Restoring 'authentically' and opening to the public the large complex that is a country house and its estate can therefore run costs into many millions of pounds; even a visitor centre, not the thing to be preserved itself but a place of gentle site indoctrination, teas and toilets, can now run up a bill of £2 million or more (Pl. 7).

Lower down the financial scale, many hundreds of thousands of pounds can be paid in compensation to an owner for *not* damaging a landscape or even just a single monument, and all over Britain lots of the last type of site, protected as Scheduled Ancient Monuments under Act of Parliament, now routinely cost the taxpayer thousands of pounds in payments to landowners and tenants to 'manage' the site sympathetically for five years.

Conservation is a more positive process, of which management agreements are an executive tool. Here, thought *is* given to the future, though not necessarily a very long one. Management is the means of securing some sort of future for parts of the surviving past by using a toolkit of statutory, professional and psychological devices, often now supported by the overt interest of an informed and vocal minority in society. Conservation Areas, for example, now numbering about seven thousand in England, are often in the public eye, not least because those who live in them have much to lose should they not be respected. Essentially they are part of the statutory provision for the vetting of development and for the expenditure of public money in enhancing an urban or residential area with an historic interest. In general, all of us now live in a world in which officials, in the name of their organisations, have legal powers to make agreements maintaining or introducing land-use regimes favourable to the perpetuation of landscape features such as buildings, streets and streetscapes in towns, skylines in London, hedges, barns and flora in the countryside – and Ancient Monuments in all three.

One of the nicest ironies of our time is that much of this anti-individual, anti-property owner's rights, collectivist provision has developed, even been enacted, during the years when we have enjoyed in Britain the most radically right-wing government this century. A basic incompatibility existed for it between that individual freedom and entrepreneurial spirit it would release on the one hand and, on the other, the sincere patriotically-fired desire to conserve a national heritage (within financial limits of course). This is now complicated by our obligations to Europe which limit our national freedom; the need for Environmental Assessments was imposed on Britain, for example, in the face of considerable government resistance. The simple fact is, however, that in general the landed heritage can only be afforded in the last resort by central government funding, that is through revenue raised by taxes (or its invisible equivalent, a value written off against Capital Transfer Tax). Though that generalisation is not absolutely true of the major non-governmental player in the field, the National Trust, it has nevertheless only been enabled to proceed with some of its major acquisitions of recent years, quite properly deemed as in the public interest, with the help of considerable public funding in several different ways.

The crucial role of central government funds, despite the thrust for greater self-reliance of the present administration, becomes even more so when conservation, rather than just preservation, is pursued. The objective changes from one of merely keeping to one of adapting to further, perhaps totally new, functions; and that can be very expensive too (though not necessarily more so than demolition and rebuilding). One has only to look at current developments in redundant dockland areas for illustration. Liverpool makes the point, and in various other respects so do the City of London, Bristol, Chester, Newcastle upon Tyne and York in England, Glasgow in Scotland, and, among many others, Boston, Massachusetts. While the cult of water in urban conservation and renewal was such a marked development of the 1980s, its sensitivity to market forces as so vividly illustrated in London's dockland in the early 1990s may inhibit further brash redevelopment. The reason is, of course, that whatever a government's political and socio-economic intentions in ploughing money into such areas, profit-making is the motive of its partners while it relies on the private sector.

We see the same principle of central government funding at work in several large areas and innumerable smaller pieces of the countryside acquired or designated for conservation in the public interest. It is channelled as grant-aid through the Countryside Commission, the Nature Conservancy Council, the National Heritage Memorial Fund and the Historic Buildings and Monuments Commission in Britain, and their many counterparts elsewhere, such as the National Park Service in the USA (Chapter 8).

Restoration is a different matter altogether. Theoretically, it is impossible, for nothing can be restored to be exactly what it was. The act of restoration itself marks a change: a shattered Greek urn meticulously restored is not the same urn as made in 300 BC. Indeed, the very skill of its contemporary restoration may well shift the emphasis of our admiration from then to now. Restoration can induce change and may indeed be carried out for that purpose, the achievement of which may itself produce further, perhaps unintended results (Pl. 8).

The restoration of HMS *Victory*, for example, began many years ago so that Nelson's flagship, though remaining in commission, could be maintained as an evocative national monument open to the public. The crowds now press through in such numbers (302,875 in 1989) that the wear and tear on the 200-year-old fabric, plus the tourist expectation of seeing the complete genuine article, have led to the implementation of a further long-term restoration programme. Its end result will be the complete *replacement* of the original structure so that we will end up with an unintended replica, a one-to-one surrogate of the vessel Nelson actually paced at the battle of Trafalgar. One might well query the rationale of this process in academic, even ethical terms, but if the crowds flock through and are satisfied with what they see, will it matter that a cultural sleight of hand, with the best intentions in the world, will nevertheless

11

have been perpetrated? Which is the more important – conservation of the original artefact for its own intrinsic historic interest, or its replacement by a visitable piece of hardware replicating a favourite item on the national menu of the British heritage? To ask the supplementary question, 'Need anyone know?' is to avoid that issue – while raising others.

Related issues were raised in 1989–90 by the National Trust's decision to restore Uppark, one of its great country houses, after a disastrous fire had gutted the roof and most of the interior but left the walls standing. The objective was and is quite clear: to restore the house as closely as possible to what it looked like the day before the fire, using original material as far as possible. Crucial in the background to the decision were two factors: the house was insured; and much of the furniture and fittings from all but the (domestically occupied) top floors had been saved or salvaged in a most remarkable operation of considerable bravery and complexity. Nevertheless, characteristically for England, 'to restore or not?' became a public issue, with many providing unsolicited advice to the Trust not to proceed. Anyway, the Trust has gone ahead with what will surely prove to be one of the most expensive 'restoration' exercises ever carried out, and doubtless the result will be utterly convincing. It will not, however, be the William and Mary house which led the Trust to acquire it for the nation in the first place; though it *will* be a magnificent monument to late twentieth-century skill and heritage reconstruction. Uppark makes a most interesting case.

For a century now, *reconstruction* has been eschewed by the official state agencies in Britain in their dealings with monuments on land. As a result we now have many splendid ruins – as Uppark could alternatively have been – visually impressive as they stand but often difficult to comprehend in their three-dimensional jumble of different building phases and changing uses. If only people in the past had kept it simple, our task would be so much simpler; but of course they changed and adapted their buildings through time just as we continue to do, for instance at Uppark. In that sense the very structural complexity of a ruined castle or monastery portrays a factual reality about the past. To restore in the face of that reality immediately involves decisions, historical, practical, ethical, about what we are to restore to. And again, the policy decision about its future having been taken, Uppark also raises such questions as its restoration proceeds.

In the case of any large country house realistically we are dealing with a centuries-long accretion of drive and inertia, of stylishness and make do and mend. Do we restore it to its original appearance in the seventeenth century, to that of any one of its successive phases such as its heyday in the 1790s, to a mixture of them so that it becomes as it never was before, or to a particular period associated with a particular inhabitant so that it becomes trapped in a time-warp? And if the last, say an especially famous person, what do we do if he or she had, by our standards, execrable taste in interior design? The authentic interior restorations for the National Trust, easily recognisable as attributable to John Fowler, have become an oft-quoted example of one sort of answer, one which we can already see to have been as much of Fowler's time earlier this century as of 'period restoration'.

Or take an outdoor site, for example the milecastle at Sewingshields on Hadrian's Wall, a World Heritage Site full of academic interest overlaid with multiple uses and ambiguities of restoration and reconstruction. There it was decided to consolidate for display features from the two main structural periods of the site's archaeology. As one of the main points of interest from its excavation was the demonstration of medieval reoccupation of a Roman frontier post, the decision was justifiable and praiseworthy, consciously not opting for the easy display of the fortlet's original form. But the result on site is visually a mess, very difficult to understand and positively misleading since the site has never looked like this before. Its appearance is a construct of the 1980s. The point is familiar but it remains worthwhile stressing that the physical appearance of the past is neither self-given nor self-evident. It is created by answering the questions above and acting accordingly.

The face of the past we see is structured, piece by piece yet unable to encompass the other 99 per cent which is not being preserved at all, never mind restored. Restoration is highly selective within a selection. Never mind, runs the argument, as long as we 'feel' a restoration to be 'right', why worry? After all, a very proper function of the past now is psycho-logical, impressionistically reinforcing in a self-perpetuating cycle popular expectation of what the visible, tangible past ought to be. The dangerous ambivalence in all this was neatly expressed by Joseph Heller (*Picture This*, 1988, Chapter 2) in remarking of a statue that 'It was an authentic Hellenistic imitation of a Hellenic reproduction ... for which there had never been an authentic original subject.'

The *re-creation* of a past can encourage such an attitude. We can con-vincingly enter the 'now' of the bogus exposed in Philip Norman's 'Age of Parody': 'The whole character of Britain in the Eighties is summed up by what has been done to the pubs' (*The Age of Parody*, 1990). It is also, however, a world of seriousness. Where motives are high, deep scholarship interplays with controlled imagination; but serious money-making can be involved too and that can shift priorities elsewhere, sometimes producing intellectual tawdriness and the physically sham.

Past introductions

Much in vogue today is playing at the past: Britaineering, Sealed Knottery, Druidic dressings up and medieval quaffing and wenchery. By and large, this is harmless, affording pleasure and at least not damaging tangible history whatever it may do to its image and, sometimes, to those involved. If it provides vicarious fun to participants, entertainment to spectators, and helps raise charitable funds, as in Ian Botham's route-march across the Alps Hannibal-style with elephants, so be it. It is probably kinder to regard such goings-on as illustrative of the stimulus of the past rather than decry them as the prostitution of history itself. The only danger is that participants and watchers dupe themselves into thinking that what they are doing *is* history.

All this activity, far from illuminating the past, is actually saying something profound and poignant about the present. A radio programme featuring the participants at 'Tudor' Kentwell (BBC Radio 4, 29 December) illustrated pathos and the very necessary therapy behind the fun and pretence. An individual dissatisfaction with uncolourful and unimportant lives is a fairly obvious part-explanation, for nothing so easily puffs up the ego as, for example, the wearing of voluminous and coded robes flaunted in ceremony. Academics and local dignitaries play the game at Congregations and Mayoral Robings, and so too the High Court every day, all of them buttressing institutions as well as self. It is but a shading down the scale, opening such opportunity to the man on the Clapham omnibus who does not have such pomp built into his daily life, to provide the setting for a week's make-believe 'historic experience' or to invent spurious 'historic' occasions involving dressing up for a Sunday afternoon's entertainment. The historical validity of the pomp and circumstance matters not one jot, and in any case the sanctity of venerability comes faster these days; once is an Event, twice and you've created a Tradition.

Beyond this marginalia of then, now, surely lies a deeper sociological significance. Is our present really so benign that challenges, particularly ones with physical risk, have to be sought in reverting to a past activity? Dressing up, even cavorting around in a carefully stage-managed medieval tourney or, less spuriously, in an exhibition of morris dancing (Pl. 9) is one thing but setting out to sail the Indian Ocean on a bundle of reeds or the north Atlantic in some bits of stitched leather is another: the indifferent sea is not to know that you are testing the practicality of historical theory, legitimate or otherwise. Here could be dragons indeed.

To dress up seems a natural urge, indulged in from childhood and nothing more than a physical expression of personal fantasy, of wishing, but perhaps not too seriously, to be someone else. The experience is temporary, enjoyed knowing you can return (Pl. 9). Doing so in a past-time context does not of itself change the nature of the act; a girl dressing up as a nurse or as Florence Nightingale is still a girl putting on different clothes and using her imagination. A possible danger when grown-ups do it is that they *do* take it too seriously. The proverbial 'little man', perhaps trapped during the week in anonymous, routine work on assembly line or office desk, can release his self by not only imagining that he is a named pikeman in Cromwell's New Model Army for the purposes of an evening's re-enactment; he can go on to delude himself that he has actually become that person and is engaged in an authentic reliving of a real, historic event. Such recreation is of course impossible; any sense of reality exists only in the contemporary delusion.

One of the touching aspects of such re-enactments is that often 'historic' means merely 'in the past', not necessarily 'of significance in the past'; thus enthusiasts 're-enact' as 'historic' minor skirmishes in the English Civil War without pretension to their being 'historic' in the sense enjoyed by the Battle of Waterloo.

Advocates of re-creation, 'living history' as it is so plausibly called, argue that, nevertheless, since the past is an intellectual construct anyway and historians cannot agree among themselves about a 'true' interpretation, any sense of 'reality' is valid in helping us to understand. The argument is phoney but it would be difficult to deny that positive benefits of such experience are perceived to exist by both creators of it and their customers. A typical advertisement, for example, reads: 'VOLUNTEERS. Join the *n*th Annual Re-Creation of Tudor Domestic Life at this HISTORIC HOUSE. Live as part of a Tudor household for 2–3 weeks ... Many roles to fill from archers, swordsmen, clerics, smiths, carpenters, etc., to musicians, cooks, spinners, weavers, needlewomen, gentry and labourers. Skills and aptitudes welcome but not essential. A stimulating and unique experience for men, women and children of all ages and walks of life.' This was the Kentwell of the BBC radio programme which provided such interesting listening (above p. 14).

History, like water, can apparently just be turned on; privatised, at places like Kentwell it may also be polluted. Educationalists, however, assert and demonstrate that, properly prepared, re-creation and re-enactment can engage children's interest in history for its own sake.

To dress up *and* do something physically demanding extends the action without necessarily increasing its validity. Especially is this so when the action is academically pointless, even spurious; such could well suggest a degree of self-indulgent, even unhealthy, escapism. Perhaps, however, we should see such exploits, real or pretend, as expressing the individual urge to be a 'hero', to go forth on a quest and return with the Tablets or the Grail, knowing that people will watch, interested, envious, hopeful. Society needs its heroes, now quite as much as then.

All this play-acting with real live people now has its counterpart in the field with real dead monuments. A very thin line indeed is drawn between restoration and re-creation, as colonial Williamsburg, Virginia, so disarmingly exemplifies. Re-creation of archaeological sites is less common in Britain (Pl. 10) and is certainly officially discouraged on the actual site. The full-size, 1987 Roman fort gateway at South Shields is an interesting, controversial exception to the practice; it required a public inquiry and the disregard of a great deal of informed archaeological evidence for the Secretary of State for the Environment to be able to give it the go-ahead.

Stonehenge, in contrast, exemplifies the results of the pursuance of the rigorously academic English tradition; more is the pity, some would say. There, only very limited re-erection of stones known to have moved in the last two centuries has been carried out; there is no re-creation. In its purest form the tradition is seen on many less well known archaeological sites: there is no re-creation, no restoration, no maintenance, and no interpretation on site of, for example, a prehistoric field system, marvellously surviving in the present landscape of, say, Dartmoor. It is a man-made structure in about as natural a state as it can be, mutely biding its way through time as best it can and as indeed it always has done (well, for three to four thousand years anyway). Or at least, that is how it appears. In fact, in some cases nowadays it *is* being maintained but through bureaucratic action rather than on-site repair.

At the other extreme, from the private sector, we have not so much the *re*-creation of what might have been as the creation of what never was. Fakes can be made of sites and buildings as well as of portable artefacts. At one site, for example, the public are privileged to see in return for their entrance fee a bogus Anglo-Saxon church based on spurious documentary evidence and the rather botched conversion of two semi-detached nineteenth-century farm cottages. Their axis turned through 90° to create a nave, their eastern gable-end embellished with a 1970s apse, their external detailing throughout was enhanced by both genuine and fake medieval architectural fragments, none of course *in situ*. This eclectic concoction is part of a privately created heritage area containing other re-creations side by side with the authentic. The casual visitor is not helped to distinguish between them and has to pay for the lot. This is dishonest and unacceptable.

Different in all respects except the basic act of re-creation in the field was the BBC's so-called but still-remembered 'Iron Age Village'. Built in 1977, destroyed in 1978, its meteoric *three*-dimensional life attempted a sort of past with really living-in, live people, here today, gone tomorrow; yet, through the medium of stored video-film, presumably destined to last *two*-dimensionally for ever. This prehistoric re-creation in the woods of Tollard Royal, Wiltshire, was not of course a deliberate fake, unlike the church; it was in fact a serious attempt at an interesting experiment, limited by its requirement to meet televisual needs and by the presence of twentieth-century people. Momentarily, right at the end of its one-year existence when the inhabitants had learnt by experience, its realisation was as authentic as we are likely to be able to attain with present knowledge. Up till then, its flaw had been the people. They bore even less resemblance to Iron Age farmers in their individual and group psychology, their cultural conditioning and their technical skills than did the volunteers at that country house to their Tudor predecessors. Whatever the producer's ambitions, the BBC was primarily interested in good television, and indeed the nation watched as its naive contemporaries struggled and floundered and generally made a meal of reinventing the wheel. The interest was human rather than archaeological; the past was used to provide an unusual setting for an otherwise familiar tale of uncountry folk in unfamiliar circumstances coping with problems and showing true British grit while so doing.

The setting may be right but we cannot create, never mind re-create, the human part of the past. Of course we can acquire past skills, rediscover lost techniques, even gain some understanding of what and how they thought; but our apparently deeply felt yearning to know what they were like, even to be like them, is doomed to failure, at its most dangerous when we imagine success.

Yet, I wonder; there is more to the past than authenticity. The above argument covers only one level of appreciation of that extraordinary Iron Age fantasy. The TV programmes aroused considerable interest; by their own terms of reference, *they* were a success. Many people probably heard of the Iron Age for the first time, perhaps had their first glimpse of its buildings, its technology, its problems. Perhaps the general educational value outweighed the phoneyness. And the people living in their 'Iron Age' learnt, by the end, to respect late prehistoric achievement; they also learnt about self-respect. Despite their initial ineptitude in Iron Age terms, they went forth on their individual journeys of exploration, stuck it out and triumphed in a way against considerable adversity. They became folk-heroes and heroines for a day; but it was twentieth-century people who showed their mettle, not Iron Age man who came off best. For of course the whole bizarre affair was not about the past at all; it was about us, now.

The episode has a sting in the tail too for, as always, there was a strain of irony, of ambivalence, in the then/now relationship so artificially created. In the first place, the volunteers accidentally and unknowingly built their farm on top of the remains of prehistoric fields, thereby achieving unwitting verisimilitude of location at the cost of damaging the very authenticity they sought to emulate. Secondly, because that location was only rented for a year, at the end the site was cleared, its house deliberately burnt down, the other structures dismantled, the whole left to nature. As a result, the site has now become one of considerable scientific interest and potential. Its floral recolonisation is being studied, its post-depositional history, in archaeological jargon, monitored. In due course the site can be archaeologically excavated and results compared with the archive carefully recorded in 1978 and now waiting a future when it is needed. A third and almost incidental ambivalence is that here I am already writing of the whole affair as history. One of the distinguishing traits of contemporary life is that, in addition to more past being available than previously, it is catching up on us more quickly than ever before.

1   The changing past, and problematical too. Stonehenge (top right), Wiltshire, and the area to its south and west from the air in the 1920s, with the remains of the 1917 Royal Flying Corps camp showing clearly in an ancient landscape pinpricked with the circles of second millennium BC burial mounds. Recent detailed archaeological surveys of what is now a World Heritage Site have significantly increased our information: for example a prehistoric settlement area lies immediately north of the RFC camp. The road west–east across the photograph is now the A303 trunk road, to be upgraded to dual carriageway in the 1990s with enormous implications for this sensitive landscape, itself the subject of ambitious plans to improve its presentation to the public.

2 The eclectic past, witnessed (December) looking north-east across the archaeologically excavated foundations of a friary church, laid out for public delectation by a heritage-conscious City Council, towards an inner-city residential development in post-modernist idiom. It echoes the Gothic architecture and cloisters of the heavily restored but medieval Blackfriars, just off the developing 'Chinatown' of Stowell Street, Newcastle upon Tyne.

3 Expensive patterns of the past: scaffolding and shadows in March at Fountains Abbey, North Yorkshire, part of a World Heritage Site and typical of the hundreds of major buildings surviving as ruins in official care which require, not restoration, but a continuous programme of maintenance and repair just to retain 'as found'.

National, municipal and family images of selected history line up (November) as monuments t Llandudno, Gwynedd, in the form of a stone circle erected in 1963 to mark the Royal National Listeddfod, a fountain commemorating the Jubilee of Queen Victoria erected by the Mostyn amily, and a nineteenth-century pier recently restored as a tourist attraction.

5 Amphibious tourists approach the most-visited heritage target in England: Tower Bridge and he Tower of London (to the right) in July.

6 Downland landscape around Avebury, Wiltshire, part of a World Heritage Site where development pressures occasioned three public inquiries 1988–90. Viewed south-east from Windmill Hill, a National Trust property on which is a series of Neolithic enclosures, the largest prehistoric mound in Europe, Silbury Hill, lies in the valley to the right in an area farmed since the fourth millennium BC. The characteristic tree-clumps on the skyline to the left cover second millennium BC burial mounds on land recently acquired by the National Trust and the subject of its current Avebury Appeal.

7 Sylvan tranquillity in classical mode: the eighteenth-century water gardens and one of the temples at Studley Royal, North Yorkshire, another World Heritage Site, in March after recent and expensive restoration by the National Trust. A new visitor centre is being built off-site and out of sight from the gardens and abbey.

8 The recycled past in compatible contemporary use: corporate lunch (June) in the sensitively restored (1980s) and awe-inspiring interior of one of the oldest timber-framed buildings (originally mid-twelfth century) still standing in Europe, Coggeshall Grange barn, Essex.

9 Playing at pastness in public, however temporary the experience, demands seriousness and vigour: morris dancers in August at the National Garden Festival, Gateshead.

10   The past on display in the form of an *in situ* reconstructed ring cairn and burial mound of the second millennium BC, part of the prehistoric cemetery now around the shores of Brenig reservoir, near Cerrig-y-Drudion, Clwyd, north Wales.

Pasts with people

Living with the past

3

'May the past be with you' could well be today's thematic intonation. Many of our yesterdays, or more correctly their influence, affect much of contemporary life, perhaps more deeply and certainly more strongly, than many people realise; and to the dismay of many of those who do realise. 'Do we want a City of London which is a vibrant financial capital or one large archaeological site?' asked Virginia Bottomley in 1989 during her brief spell as Minister in the Department of the Environment; unappreciative that her choice was limited to the former since the latter is a fact of life. Was she in fact asking the right question? Or even a justifiable question? Of what was she fearful? Is the unavoidable fact of such a heritage necessarily at odds with contemporary needs? Is it only archaeology which is a block to contemporary physical development or is a more general historical blockage at work too? And why should a Minister of State or we care anyway?

Caring or not, a lot of people are now interested in the past one way or another; and whereas it used to be mainly academics, also in one form or another, now the interest takes all sorts of forms, consuming various sorts of pasts which can be used, for example, as a trigger for making money – or not, as the case may be. Passing my neighbourhood branch of W. H. Smith's recently, I glanced as usual at the stand of 'Bargain Books'. The pressing horde of publications none of us really quite want contained items predictably on cookery, decorating, furry animals and birds, your body, travel, sport, sewing and gardening; and a lurid infestation of *Blytoniana E*. There were also 'history' books, the following being a complete list of the titles on offer in this field:

History of World War II: ed. in chief A. J. P. Taylor, comp. S. L. Mayer
  (Macdonald 1988, Black Cat imprint, £7.99)
Illustrated London News Marching to War 1933–39: intro. M. Gilbert
  (Fellow, Merton College, Oxford) (Bestseller 1989)
The Country Life Book of The Living History of Britain: The story

of Britain's history, its heritage and the formation of its landscape: consultant W. G. V. Balchin (Midsummer, 3rd imp. 1988, £12.99)

History of Golf: M. Williams (Galley 1988, £6.99)

The Illustrated History of Helicopters: M. Heatley (Bison, reprint 1990, £5.95)

The Pictorial Treasury of Classic Steam Trains: N. Huxtable (Bison 1989, £9.99)

Treasures of Lords: T. Rice (Willow 1989, £7.95)

The Care and Repair of Antiques: A comprehensive fully illustrated guide to the care and repair of almost any antique (Swallow 1990, £6.99)

And to ram home the point that the popular past really is a foreign country with its own currency and not the 'history' controlled by academic historians and archaeologists, across the mall Our Price was promoting 'The definitive history of the Rolling Stones on video'.

Simultaneously, the British Prime Minister, totally unaware of what was in store for her from this very issue, was defending her government's attitude towards Europe in the wake of the resignation of the Secretary of State for Trade and Industry. As is now well-known history, he had referred to Germans in a fairly uncomplimentary way reflecting anachronistic views rooted in British experience of two World Wars in one generation; or so it was being argued by those over-reacting to the publication of actually quite widely-held prejudices. Mrs Thatcher, then the Prime Minister, informed the House of Commons that she, together with the German Chancellor and the Labour MP for Wallsend, agreed about 'the wisdom of learning from the study of history'. The phrase '*study* of history', not just 'history' itself, is particularly interesting, both in its own right and in coming from someone whose own understanding of the subject, deriving presumably from 'study', led her during the bicentennial celebrations of the French Revolution in 1989 to opine that that event was possibly of marginal significance.

On the same day (17 July) that 'the study of history' was being given the imprimatur of Prime Ministerial approval in the context of Anglo-German relations forty-five years after the end of World War II, *The Independent* carried an item in its '1940 Revisited' series headlined 'Hitler activates plan to invade England' and, on the same page, printed a photograph showing 'A sandwich board man advertising the Cabinet War Rooms, Churchill's underground command centre, near the Palace of Westminster yesterday', fifty years to the day when Hitler moved to invade Britain. A certain ambivalence seemed to be at play here.

The War Rooms, now one of the tourist sights of London (Pl. 11), are open to the public as part of Britain's heritage; or are they merely an illustration of that 'history' from the study of which we are to learn and presumably benefit? Learn what? Benefit whom? Whether educational or merely entertainment, these Rooms mutated from real-life war command centre to curiositie heritage centre well within the lifetimes of millions who lived through the years of Nazi threat. They and their children are charged for entry as is to be expected in a Britain tagged by its detractors as a place now where everything is priced and nothing is valued for its own sake. To call it 'the enterprise culture' is another way of saying the same thing but from a different point of view.

There would seem to be some points worth considering in this contemporary *mélange*. What is this thing 'history', trundled out at Prime Ministerial level as worthy material for our learning curves and yet apparently trivialised, at least as a concept, in cut-price books about helicopters and golf? Are the physical remains, the archaeology, of a key place in the defence of Britain at its greatest hour of external threat, and a book about hitting a small white ball around the countryside, of the same *genus*? How does one reconcile the preparation for public consumption of a monument to very specifically anti-German effort, and then its aggressive promotion as a marketable asset to the international tourist trade, with simultaneous political effort across the street and in the media to play down anti-German sentiments? And how justified is the suspicion that such sentiments, however maladroit in their timing and career terms, at the very least genuinely voiced an element in the British view of Europe? Does an 'age factor' come into play here too, the residence of such supposed sentiments being mainly among the over-forties, that segment of the population which, having *inter alia* survived the War against Hitler, is now so important to the domestic leisure industry?

That there is a chauvinistic element in the British psyche is beside the point here, though of course chauvinism itself, and indeed nationalism, both contain powerful ingredients from selective pasts. Even the Cabinet War Rooms are not politically neutral. Their presentation may be historically factual and interpretatively correct, but only within an unstated framework of various assumptions about the nature of history as seen from central London in the late 1980s. Similarly, the anti-British glorification of independence American-style in the introductory video-presentation of Williamsburg, Virginia, would hardly seem to be designed to contribute to the present peace of nations, let alone a 'special relationship'. Yet, perhaps curiously, at the two extremes of personal and international relations, such chauvinistic hype does not seem to have any effect. Perhaps both, and their many counterparts, belong from their moment of inception to the history of heritage rather than to that history itself which is deserving of study. But then, what is history if not selective itself which is deserving of study. But then, what is history if not selective interpretation of the past?

It does not exist, complete, pure and neutral, as some total abstract entity from which any two people wanting to know about, say, Anglo-German relations in the twentieth century either AD or BC, would remove the same two self-defining chunks. Academically, this of course is one of the truisms of the study of the past, a truism nevertheless which seems seldom to be grasped, in public affairs especially. Learning, in the sense of understanding, history is therefore difficult enough; learning the lessons of it begs as many questions as the process may seek to answer. Not least, any answers sought will depend on the questions asked, and they themselves depend on a multitude of factors apparently secondary to the primary quest. For example, what is the nature and availability of primary evidence, the state of research in the field being interrogated, and the cultural conditioning, the brief and the competence of the interrogator?

A Prime Minister may, nevertheless, legitimately consult a group of scholarly historians to discuss Germany in the twentieth century but, as the 'leaked' document recording such a discussion showed, while both consensus and differences emerged (as one would expect), two other vital factors contributed to the exercise. One was the interpretation of the discussion enshrined in the record of the meeting. This record immediately itself became an historical document, both for its own sake as a record and as the instigator of a minor political incident in which both the sources of the Prime Minister's advice and the reason for the confidential document arriving in the hands of the press were questioned.

The other was the *use* that the Prime Minister could make of the results of the occasion. As well as noting the results as recorded through the filtering agency of the mind of her secretary, she would naturally put her own personal and political interpretations on the significance of the historical interpretations to which she had listened (with what amount of understanding, of prejudice?), and *still* have to make her own judgements as to when and how to use whatever it was she thought herself to have derived from the occasion. There is nothing unusual whatsoever in this process; we are all engaged in it much of the time, and the example is taken merely as a current and well-publicised one, albeit involved with issues rather grander than our daily ones. Interestingly for this author, *The History Debate*, 'A History Today Book', independently seized on the same occasion to ask questions about the nature of history in an 'Introduction' which seems from internal evidence to have been finalised about the time that this chapter was first written.

'Thatcher meets the historians' is a little story which well illustrates that 'learning the lessons of history' is not only a complex exercise but one so fraught with difficulties that the chances are fairly high not so much of learning nothing as of learning the wrong lessons. Even that assumes that there are any lessons at all in history. At a technical level, there clearly are in the sense that, once someone had invented the wheel, for example, there is no need for anyone else to do so again (though that clearly is one lesson we have not learnt); but there is absolutely no guarantee in dealing with collective human behaviour that what has happened once will happen again. Nevertheless, the irony is that, in consulting the past as we all do all the time in attempts to anticipate the future, we may for all we know actually be interfering in, and inhibiting, a process which *might* at the very least contain an element of repetition.

The recent opening to the public of the Cabinet War Rooms provides a very simple example (at £3.50 adult, £1.75 child, entrance fee for twenty-one historic rooms which include that from which Churchill telephoned Roosevelt across the Atlantic). Despite the apparently anti-German nature of this addition to the recent history industry, might it not actually be just one of many contributions to the current groundswell of hope that inter-state, but essentially civil, war in Europe is finally over? By designating the Rooms as heritage, we have effectively consigned them to the past, implying not only that they are of interest as a monument to a phase of national history but also that they are now redundant and will not be needed again. Technically, that is certainly true but that is hardly the point: the Rooms could well convey a symbolism about past foolishness rather than current chauvinism. Over and above their use by Churchill and his colleagues, and whatever was in the minds of those deciding to bring this hitherto secret installation into the public arena as an archaeological site, in a sense it now has, in the 1990s, an added value. It is an unconscious monument to the archaism of those Ridleyesque views which so suddenly brought about the downfall of a Cabinet Minister. Essentially, he was forced to resign not so much for history's sake itself but for promulgating a particular interpretation of history which, whether correct or not in a scholarly sense, was, at that moment, politically maladroit. With a further twist of the past's political knife, ironically the Prime Minister who sacked him, however reluctantly, was herself lanced by Europa on her post-Roman way towards resignation. 'Then, now' indeed.

If Mr Ridley and Mrs Thatcher unconsciously found themselves in a fifty-year-old time-warp, their confusion can to an extent be understood. Throughout 1990, Britain wallowed in a miasma of semi-centennial anniversaryism of simpler times when the Hun was clearly the foe and Britain's Gallic neighbours were once again exhibiting their knavish unreliability. Perhaps such flag-waving and communal remembrance would have happened anyway, for these things require quite a long lead-time to organise, but one wonders if the celebrations did not contain an element of nationalist reaction to galloping Europeanisation and, in particular, to the self-glorying over-the-top panache of the French Revolution bicentennial in 1989. The British celebration a year earlier of its nearest equivalent, the so-called 'Glorious Revolution' of 1688 which brought a Dutchman to the throne was, on reflection and in comparison, decidedly low-key and not at all blessed with official flamboyance. Perhaps the anniversary was a little too full of ambivalences for outright celebration, either popular or Establishment. Far easier to do the obvious and celebrate a clear-cut black and white event in which, with little ambiguity, the English once again did what they believe themselves to be good at, to whit thumping foreigners. So the defeat of the Spanish Armada in 1588, while an event of considerable national significance but of little moment beyond, was duly marked with festive chauvinism – as Spain was fast emerging as an active partner of Britain in the new, economic community of collaborative Europe.

In 1990 Britain could, riposting to France's 1989 excesses, do what the French could not and that is celebrate the continued existence of its Royal family. The point was central to a 1990 two-part TV thriller, called 'Never Come Back' but repeated by the BBC in December, which was based on the idea that fifty years earlier elements in the British Establishment loyal to Edward VIII were able to dangle before collaborative French eyes the carrot of royalty in the possibility of the re-enthronement of an ex-king. The main 1990 British anniversary, however, was the half-century of the Battle of Britain, providing another opportunity of not too gently reminding our cross-Channel neighbours that 'A Nation at Bay', as *The Daily Telegraph* called its celebratory Battle of Britain supplement (16 June), was brought to this parlous state in part at least because of French deficiencies. Funnily enough, the French did not seem to see it that way for, at the same time, the Paris Métro was plastered with giant posters of de Gaulle in various guises but essentially as saviour of France from 1940 onwards. Understandably, the synchronous half-century of the man who actually became head of the (Vichy) French state in 1940, Marshal Pétain, was currently being ignored. Presumably the assumption was that, despite the similarity of the task now compared to then, the circumstances, objectives and likely results were completely different from those fifty years ago as questioned by the British Secretary of State for Trade and Industry.

If de Gaulle nevertheless saved France in 1940, as seen by a successful republican state in 1990, Britain's rescue act was on an altogether higher plane. In saving itself, almost incidentally Britain engaged in a Battle upon which, as Churchill said at the time and as the *Telegraph* was ready to quote at the start of its feature now, 'depends the survival of Christian civilisation'. His was of course a marvellous speech, and the celebration of the context now has at least brought it back into circulation to a new generation familiar, if at all, with Churchillian rhetoric not as the words of a man of the hour in desperate straits, but more as the subject of rather tired parody (most recently by the former Minister of Administrative Affairs in BBC TV's 'Yes, Prime Minister').

It was a little difficult to decipher the signals coming out of the Battle of Britain anniversary celebrations. On the one hand, the fifty years since then have shown that it was one of the very last genuinely decisive military occasions when it was basically down to the Brits. Even though some doubt exists now as to whether Hitler really would have invaded had the RAF failed, popular perception at the time was of imminent invasion. On the other hand, none of those engaged at a critical time in building the new collaborative Europe of the 1990s wants too much nationalism or anti-German/Italian sentiment stoked up merely through the accident of the passing of fifty years. While it was almost bizarre in a sense to observe, at least in the popular press, the extent to which the 1940s (with a touch of the Falklands) were fought out again during the Football World Cup in *Italia 90,* the occasion curiously also had the effect of providing an acceptable surrogate at a moment of national sensitiveness inevitably stimulated by personal memories and official anniversaryism.

One of the intellectual journalists of the Sunday press went further. Michael Ignatieff (O, 8 July) recognised that the qualities of pluck, determination and so on used to describe the English team in its match against Germany 'were coined in the Battle of Britain' and that, in his own reactions (despite being a Canadian), 'tribal atavism was at work'; but he nevertheless had the presence of mind in watching other games to 'wonder whether four centuries of European history had actually happened. The battles of the Reformation and Counter-Reformation [were] still being fought out on the playing fields of Italy. It [was] still northern, Protestant Europe, efficient and industrious, versus southern Europe.' That may or may not have struck people listening to the TV commentaries at moments when excitement mounted; nevertheless maybe we were willing fodder, conscious or otherwise, as a fantasy derived from past group experience temporarily unbalanced the mundaneness of most daily life. 'The World Cup [was] a day-trip away from reality' concluded Ignatieff; just like going to Alton Towers, Frontierland or the Metro-Centre is intended to be, one might add.

It is incidentally interesting that, to make his point, Ignatieff expanded the further boundary of history backwards to the sixteenth century in a journalistic world to which 'the past' is characteristically anything in the twentieth century earlier than its middle. Such antiquity may, as appropriate, be acknowledged to have been preceded by 'Victorian'; but only if it is absolutely necessary to indicate anything before that is an earlier-ness admitted, referring to it of course in soft-focus terms like 'ancient' or 'bygone' times, depending on the newspaper and its target audience.

Meanwhile, readers of the *Telegraph* could obtain their set of twelve limited edition prints of 'Scenes of Battle' by sending their order and £1,200 to the RAF Benevolent Fund. The artist, an 'aviation archae-ologist', opened a museum in 1988 at Shoreham 'with the object of assembling a visual record of some of the air battles that were fought over south-east England ... during 1940'. This intertwining of the past in the present, and for the various facets of the present to become so entwined and in such curious cross-patterning, seems a very contemporary phenomenon. Just as it so struck Patrick Wright returning to England after a prolonged absence and finding his return enmeshed in a country besotted and befixed by the raising of the *Mary Rose* in 1985, so on a smaller scale but equally strikingly was I reduced to psychological pap on returning from my first visit to the foreign past in South America. On yet another fine 1990 Saturday (15 September), the operation of Heathrow International Airport was suspended for ten minutes while the Battle of Britain commemorative flypast staggered overhead. Finding the visuals of little interest, I watched the people: their emotional reactions were both moving and incredible, clearly stimulated by surges of personal memories and the iconographic values of the amazingly small flying machines chugging into the distance; but, boy oh boy, was I or was I not aware of being back in my native land of yesteryear?

Spitfires in the blue skies of that fine June of 1940 may now be merging into one of the strongest of traditional British idylls. Britons love their summers, perhaps because of the contrast with the winters, or it may be truer to say they are in love with the *idea* of summers that once were, at least in memory, and which might be once again. Summer idylls entwine themselves round sea and scenery, nostalgia and the countryside. The love affair with the countryside in summer is particularly strong; gardens, hay-meadows, lakes, streams, rivers and hills make a powerful *potpourri*, especially when mixed up with picnics and teas of the sort provided so expertly in settings so appropriate by the National Trust. History, or at least a sense of historicalness, often comes into such idylls, and no matter how hard the entrepreneurs try with their phoney half-timbering and tacky horse-brass substitutes servicing motorways and suburban affluence, there *is* no substitute for the rural authentic. Certainly this is true of the visible setting, whether one is sipping *sirop* at the Chalet des Îles 'midst a manicured landscape in the Bois de Boulogne or being greenly vegetarian at Stone's restaurant steeped in the vernacular of sarsens and musty Tithe Barn at Avebury, Wiltshire. But tangible, visible historicity is one thing; the information environment seems to matter less.

Looking for nice places to stay, the *Sunday Times Magazine* (24 June), for example, waxed lyrical about staying at the Lobster Pot Hotel, Mousehole, Cornwall. It described the harbour 'protected by encircling granite walls so old that they may have stood there since the Phoenicians came to trade for tin ...'. Its very proper caution about the date of the harbour walls (perhaps partly medieval at earliest) is rather undermined by the implied statement of fact about the Phoenicians. There is absolutely no evidence whatsoever that any Phoenicians came to Cornwall, trading for tin or anything else, at any time. That applies even in the vaguely undefined past of the quotation in which 'since the Phoenicians' equals 'very old but it does not matter exactly when'. That said, however, the hoariness of the Phoenician tin-trader myth is such that the myth has acquired the status of 'history', rather like the popularly supposed and perpetuated blades on the wheels of Boudicca's chariot, equally fictitious. Both exemplify a part of a general perception of that which makes up English history to the extent that certain items are popularly thought of as 'history' even when they are not; and the journalistic prose quoted above merely reflects this awareness, rather than deliberately promulgating spurious history. This is very easy to do, especially if one is not consciously writing history in the sense of working towards some understanding of the original evidence but using 'history' towards some other end. In this case, the aim is a personalised account of 'the perfect weekend retreat ... above all, unforgettable'. Let's remember the address and forget the history; perhaps the dubiousness of the latter, in some sort of 'real' sense, does not matter all that much.

As an academic, however, I would argue that it does matter. Giving bogus information like that is the equivalent in the time dimension of stating in the space dimension that Bristol is 100 miles east of London. The statement is blatantly wrong and an article containing such misleading information would be rightly castigated. It might be more difficult to aspire to proper accuracy in the temporal dimension but that is no excuse; there is simply a less rigorous approach in popular usage to the basics of history than to geography, perhaps because it does not seem to matter as much. But one can become as seriously lost mentally by following misleading temporal signposts as by following inaccurate directions on a physical journey.

In the same article, for example, the caption describes the archaeologically well-known Ardaiseig crannog, Argyll, as 'an ancient man-made island' (which is correct, though greater precision about its date is easily available), 'on which a solitary Druid would once have lived'. That second statement, however, is romantic balderdash flying in a most unprofessional way in the face of all the available evidence. If I wrote 'The Ardanaiseig Hotel, Wales, from which this view of the crannog is taken, is only open at weekends to single parent families', I would be guilty of inaccurate and deliberately misleading reportage verging on fantasy; yet similar unchecked fantasy about the past splurges forth daily without blush. Not that mere inaccuracy is confined to describing the past; another caption in the same *Magazine* beneath a photograph of typical chalk downland landscape reads 'Chalk downland in Gloucestershire is good walking country', a dubious exhortation in view of the total absence of such a geological commodity in that county.

Nevertheless, it is again interesting to note in passing the significant role of the past, and specifically archaeology, in the ten 'best walks' selected as part of the delectation of summer by the *Sunday Times*. The Cotswold Way, it of the non-chalk downland, omits the time dimension, sufficient attraction presumably being hinted at in its dubbing as the 'poshest path'. Several members of the Royal family sometimes reside in the vicinity. The 'Most Roman-esque' path is along Hadrian's Wall which 'runs from the watery wasteland of Bowness-on-Solway to the appropriately named Wallsend . . .' (Pl. 12). The clichés can be forgiven, however, for at least he ends the Wall in the correct place; many journalists put the eastern end at either Newcastle or South Shields. The Ridgeway qualifies as the 'Most historic' path as it 'is one of the country's, if not the world's, most ancient routes' with lots of evidence of bygone days ('ah, 'twas a wunnerful time, bygone time'); while a walk round Rydal Water beside a house owned by Wordsworth and along the 'old coffin road' is the 'Most poetic'. A 'path of the coffin carriers' (inevitably a dead end) also features in the Lyke Wake Walk across the Yorkshire Moors; and deceased railway lines make for relatively easy walking in two National Parks, the North York Moors and the Peak. Even on the 'Windiest' walk, around St Ann's Head on the Pembrokeshire Coastal Path, 'You'll see the lighthouse where Henry Tudor, later Henry VII, landed from France in 1485 . . .'. Surprising, in this breezy context, that he is not described as 'bluff' King Hal.

If you cannot face one of these striding walks, you could try 'an underground wriggle . . . at Gough's Cave . . . where they discovered the oldest complete skeleton in 1903, so you never know what you may come across'. The archness makes one squirm rather than wriggle, though it is appropriate to the high-profile commercial exploitation of Cheddar. Doubtless 'Cheddar Man' would turn in his grave if he could. That was the name given to a Cave skeleton when it was thought to be of a very early hominid. Some twenty years ago he was dated to only *c*. 7000 BC, far too late to justify his claims to fame but nevertheless a useful date for the whole assemblage of scientific evidence from one of the most important Upper Palaeolithic cave sites in Britain (deemed not worth mentioning by, even if known to, our walking correspondent).

Correctly reported or not, history, archaeology, a sense and expectation of pastness, seemingly play a significant part in the summer idyll, whether it's a 'room with a view', a day out, or a whole holiday. In the same *Magazine,* for example, devoted to *The Pleasures of Summer* with the offending crannog in the centre of the outside front cover, the past appears mostly strongly in 'Diversions' (and perhaps its true role is merely to divert), a selection of appropriate things to do in realising the summer idyll. The Burry Man of South Queensferry near Edinburgh has been sauntering around the place on the second Friday of August since 1687 ('bar a century or so between 1865 and 1971'; in other words, a modern revival) and is clearly an obvious choice for a summer visitor, being manifestly 'ancient' (never mind the date, just sense the antiquity), palpably curious (marvel at his weirdness, never mind an explanation), and conveniently located in what is now a dramatically situated place dwarfed by the two Forth Bridges.

Even older, at least in documented history, are the herds of mute swans at Abbotsbury, Dorset: records of them 'date back to 1393 but Benedictine monks were probably keeping colonies behind Chesil Bank for centuries before then'. That such swans exist now, and are promoted as a tourist attraction, are facts, as doubtless is the statement that evidence of their keeping begins in 1393; whether any basis exists for the surmise about the swans and the monks before then (the Benedictine abbey was founded in the mid-eleventh century) hardly matters to present enjoyment of seeing the birds, but of course the insertion of the surmise gives a certain authenticity, spurious or not, to throw-away description.

From floating swans to 'A floating island which once supported a whole Bronze Age village ...' is but a short paddle for the travel journalist and the eclecticism of 'Diversions'. Like every other archaeological excavation in progress which happens to get into the papers, this one at Flag Fen near Peterborough 'is one of the most exciting archaeological sites currently being explored ...'. Unlike most others, the site actually justifies the tag, both in terms of the provision for visitors and the academic significance of the work. Pity it's not at Abbotsbury though: the project director's name is Pryor. Now that would have been worth mentioning.

An appeal to the appeal of the past is not of course confined in contemporary life to such trivial matters as holiday pursuits. It is very present not least in 'real' working life; or at least it can be thought to be helpful in imaging that 'reality', as is or as wished for.

Greenwich, for example, in common with many other employers, 'is proud of its past, and constantly thinking of its future' (advertisement, G, 10 July). A typical Janus-like pose, that, putting the past up front, believing it to be attractive to potential employees, in this case probationary schoolteachers; while, at the same moment almost, turning in the other direction just in case the reader thinks you are only backward-looking. Greenwich is able to gild its pastness with some classic name-dropping, a sort of palaeo-party trick: Henry VIII, Elizabeth I, Charles I (no mention of what happened to him) and II (or him), Christopher Wren, Inigo Jones and Samuel Pepys are all listed, the implication being presumably that they too began their careers in the Royal Borough; though their connection is not actually specified. Never mind, 'History, charm and character', presumably as represented on the Thames water-front (Pl. 13), 'make for an environment that is more than pleasant, but Greenwich Council isn't content to rest on the laurels of its past'. It therefore invites new teachers to join 'a teaching service which sets standards both now and for the future', etc., etc. in standard advertese.

The real reality of early 1990s Britain is, of course, that however elegant the verbiage and generous the '£500 settling-in allowance', teachers are leaving the profession in thousands. Furthermore, few new teachers are likely to be able to afford to buy a house in the Borough, even though half of it appeared to be up for sale, at 1988 prices of course, in the depressed property market of summer 1990.

That phenomenon is but one facet of a general disillusionment about both rural and urban living brought to light in several reports and surveys during 1990. The Civic Trust, one of the more august bodies on the preservation scene ('Britain's prim environmental watchdog' according to I, 14 August) commissioned an *Audit of the Environment,* intended to discover first of all what people felt about where they live and especially about their judgements of the quality of life in cities. The relevance of this to the past in contemporary society is that, fairly predictably but neatly documented, it showed that 'The British have a vision of the cities they want to live in', summarised by *The Independent* as 'small, green and clean ... and nice small shops in which jolly butchers in boaters and striped aprons say things like "Top of the morning to you, sir". In other words, a Civic Trust, National Trust world where the twentieth century is kept at bay.' A problem here is that this 'urban' vision seems hopelessly muddled with its rural counterpart (Pl. 14).

Maybe that is unfair to the two Trusts but doubtless over two million of their members, and many others, would respond by asking 'And what is wrong with that?' – as mother collects junior from one school by car, fills up the boot in the vast car park of the town centre supermarket, completes the car-load by meeting the teenagers off the school bus, and has the much-travelled convenience meal on the table when father arrives back in the other car from the railway station. Which came first? – present reality of traffic-choked, fume-filled, and dangerous streets or the dream of that other world based mainly in a vaguely once-was rather than a what-will-be. Given that English towns have never been 'small, green and clean' simultaneously – read Dickens, Chaucer or even archaeological reports of urban excavations – the understandable yearning is for a myth, produced by the history of urban living but nevertheless a myth.

Attempts to create that myth have of course been made, as on seemingly philanthropic 'model' estates like Saltaire, near Bradford, in the nineteenth century, and by laying out 'garden cities' in the Hertfordshire countryside of the earlier twentieth century. Today, the newspapers are full of opportunities for people to buy their way into that myth. They can, if they believe the advertising, live green and clean and still have all the mod. con. of urban living, on new estates fringing – and in some cases it's a fringe several miles wide – genuine, often old, urban centres. But, of course, such opportunities, precisely because they play to a myth, all too often prove, to use *The Independent*'s headline, 'a far cry from the Toy Town of our dreams'.

One reason is that such places are not towns, at least in the European sense refined by two and a half thousand years of urban experience. Their failure to realise their proclaimed urban character is not because of their location but because they do not have the critical mass, which includes functions as well as mere size, to be urban. Another reason for dis-illusionment with both urban living and, all too often, attempts to improve it by greenery, is equally historical. If anything, it is also more complex. Behind it, again paradoxically, lies a continuity of successful urban living over two thousand years in Western Europe; yet it too is heavily mixed up with myth, this time of 'the rural idyll'.

This is palpably present in all sorts of facets of contemporary living, as the past, or a fantasy selection from it, merges into and indeed influences the present. The Countryside Bookshop, for example, opened 'at the uncompromisingly urban address of 39 Goodge Street, London W1' (*The Bookseller*, 1 June). It 'hopes to cash in on the "great interest" that Londoners have in the countryside. ... The shop is attractively fitted in dark oak wainscoting, and it stocks titles on every aspect of country life from bird-watching to brewing and historic houses to herbal gardens.' Written in London about a view from London, that just about gives as good a definition of the present urban view of the countryside as you could find. It is of course about 'country living', the concept promoted by urban-based media for middle-class townees, and not about 'country life' as actually lived by the great majority of people in the past and still a daily experience for those working the land.

A different facet of the same past-based fantasy is illustrated in a different medium through the Laura Ashley package. Interestingly for 'past nowness', I hesitate to use the example, for 'Ashleyism' has itself already become a cliché in the history of the heritage business (and now, furthermore, with overtones of personal tragedy and socio-economic sadness in mid-Wales where another reality, economic recession, has curtailed production). Nevertheless, the particular Ashley product of interior design as well as women's clothes *is* interesting as a sociological phenomenon, both for itself, because it was commercially successful and because of its enormous influence.

It harks back from an urban viewpoint not just to a rural underpinning of a former life-style but to assumptions about, a reading of, social hierarchies and the mores that went with it. 'I did not set out to be Victorian but it was a time when people lived straightforward, balanced lives, when everything was clear-cut and respectable', said Ashley. Of course, if you believe that, anything is possible, but the vital point for present purposes is precisely that this highly selective, unrounded interpretation of (which part of?) the Victorian period was *believed to be correct*. Tellingly, as a reviewer of her biography judged, 'It was in Wales that Laura could escape the "brash newness of Thirties London Suburbia" and enter the world of late Victorian security "where neither moral values nor furniture had changed much in the previous fifty years".' The domestic décor for many a happy family and the sartorial appearance of many women over the last twenty-five years owe a great deal to the symbolism, picked up by Ashley thirty years earlier in rural Wales, of ' "family, chapel, cleanliness and orderliness; a very simple combination" ' programmed for people who ' "never went anywhere, other than for long walks, nor did anything exciting" '. The Ashley package both expresses what for her was an ideal and provides the medium for those bent on their prime objective ' "to raise families, have gardens and live life as nicely as they could" '.

Paradoxically, this notably a-religious, pre-Thatcherite vision of life 'then' as a basis for living now was apparently founded on an even more fundamental belief about a much older style of country living. 'Men should be the hunters, women are keepers of the hunters', said Laura Ashley, drawing into contemporary daily life a ten thousand and more year-old tradition which now rarely surfaces except as the cartoonist's cliché.

Most people since the Upper Palaeolithic (the later, post-glacial phase of the cartoonist's 'Old Stone Age', beginning c. 10,000 BC) have lived in what we call 'the countryside'. They, however, did not think of their environment in such terms. The phrase 'living on the land' is more appropriate to their situation and perceptions, at least as we conceive their condition. That men hunted can hardly be doubted, though their exclusivity in this food-quest would now be questioned by the feminist view of prehistory. Be that as it may, the primacy of hunting and collecting as the basic source of food gave way to food-production. This new agricultural way of life was already some four thousand years old by the time of the Roman Empire in the West, older still east of Rome. So European communities were deeply rooted in the rural landscape when, in Britain initially in the eighteenth century and thereafter increasingly and much more extensively, people from that background left it for unfamiliar territory. Their environment changed as they moved not just into industrial work to become part of a depersonalised labour force but also became wage-dependent in a market system divorced from the land around them. Their new situation, aggravated in many places by appalling working and living conditions, demanded a psychological adjustment as well as many more practical changes. Some nineteenth-century novelists – Dickens, Hardy, Mrs Gaskell – understood this, and brought it out well.

It is hardly surprising, therefore, given this lightly-sketched background, that in the new urban conglomerations a yearning for 'country life' developed. Nor is it unexpected that, in developing, it gradually came to create and accrete its own mythology, i.e. that country life was 'good'. Ironically, as so often in a present's relationship with its past, the consolidation of this urban-based cult of the rustic in the second half of the nineteenth century coincided with agricultural depression, an impoverished and decreasing rural population, and the heyday, in counterpoint, of the all-powerful local landowner. The phenomenon, manifested then, for example, in working-class bicycling, William Morris, and the formation of the National Trust itself, remains all-powerful now, forever holding twofold promise. One is practical: that life in the country is simply better, e.g. in its healthiness, uncrowdedness and quiet, relative to that suffered by the benighted town-dweller; and, second, that in some vaguely mysterious way it is better at a higher, almost philosophical level, offering to its participants such life-enhancing virtues as sturdiness, moral fibre and a naturally imbued wisdom. If you happen to have a Barbour, two retrievers, a Range-Rover, a svelte companion of the opposite sex, an angular face with sleeked-back hair and a small country estate with a

400 (at least)-year-old ancestry, it will of course also provide you with a certain 'class'.

The tide, however, is turning. Various articles and books in 1990 once more flagged a phase of growing disillusionment with the rural idyll. This time it is underscored by the strains of the consequences of expensive housing and incompatible life-styles juxtaposed in the apparently not-so-cavalier rustic community. Stephen Pile (*Weekend T, 30* June) wittily remarked on the phenomenon in welcoming two of the books about it, *A Place in the Country* and *Family Piles*. 'Apparently', he opined, 'our townie brothers have moved down there [into the country] and ruined everything ... we now have a naff, toytown rural England full of urban refugees re-creating some non-existent idyll. Spiritually you might as well tarmac the place over and call it Surbiton ... traditional rural values and eccentricities have been dumped by the middle-class new arrivals who now run everything.'

'Idealistic incomers, who have bought into their idyll', observed the author of *A Place ...,* 'naturally resist the idea that the integrated village community is a thing of the past'; the author of *Piles* remarked on the '"con-trick" of the countryside with its phoney image of cottages and cows in fields and bluebells in woods'. His last chapter is called 'Moving Out'; in it 'a happy return to London is described'. Both, says Pile, 'make a useful contribution to destroying the absurd rural myth that addles the English brain'. Witness, he might have added, the *Country Diary of an Edwardian Lady* phenomenon and the repeated attempts to find the right formula to peddle the myth in commercially successful magazines.

These two strains, urban and rural, overt in so much advertising, are implicit at a fundamental level in the British way of life, perhaps with particular assiduity in England but lurking in other countries too. Cheshire-cat-like, they merge and separate, oppose and coalesce, the 'place-in-the-country' dream of the fraught town-dweller becoming the private hell of the lonely mother frightened by things that go bump in the night, the country widow's suburban residential home proving a trap defined by social desert and an uncrossable main road where cars go faster on passing that demeaning warning sign which shows two geriatrics. Both sorts of expectations, of the improved town life, green and clean, and of the rustic Nirvana, even greener and cleaner, are proper aspirations and long may they be pursued; but, powerful motivators both, they are available to influence us today, as individuals and communally, because they genuinely emerge from our long history. Yet, simultaneously, they innocently peddle a myth. Again, there is a paradox here: historically, neither urban nor rural living has been particularly pleasant for most people, so for us to quest something that never was is truly to pursue a myth; yet those two myths are now themselves 'historical' in that over many years now both have motivated many and been found by a few. Clearly we have to live not only with a past that actually was but also with one that never occurred.

4 | *Celebrating the past*

To 'have a good time' is one of the most popular of intentions; the passage of time provides many occasions for so doing. Whether the past is being used as an excuse for a party, or whether the occasion is the medium for a genuine celebration of pastness remembered, usually at a fixed moment in time, is sometimes a moot point, but perhaps not a particularly important one.

Compulsive anniversaryism now seems characteristic of 'the heritage age' in which we live: 1990 witnessed dozens of past-related celebrations nationally and countless others at local level, and many such have already been announced for 1991. We celebrate ourselves, our organisations, our places, our heroes (Pl. 15), sometimes our authentic, significant history; we even celebrate celebrations and commemorate disasters. That deemed worthy of official national celebration comes from a very filtered sort of history, essentially patriotic, conservative and suitable for the national history curriculum (Pl. 16); we celebrated in 1990 the defeat of the Luftwaffe with lights in the sky but somehow forgot to light bonfires in seventh centennial 'celebration' of Edward I's expulsion of the Jews.

Lists of potential anniversaries are assiduously drawn up in anticipation, and carefully studied; they range from one year to thousands of years since something or other happened, from births and deaths to battles, books and discoveries. Their 'potential' relates not to whether they will happen or not as a function of time but to whether or not they should 'happen' in the form of public celebration. Nowadays, that decision seems to depend on judgements of 'worthwhileness' as much to do with contemporary politics and commerce as of the person or event on the list. Many, for example, are thinking hard now about how to handle the politics of the unavoidable four-hundredth celebration of the 'discovery' of America in 1992; equally others will be thinking 'We've got to have an event: what can we celebrate? Where's that list?' The English Tourist

Board's decision to 'celebrate' in 1991 the birth of Henry VIII smacks of that variety.

Perhaps not unnaturally for an island race, Britons are constantly inter-weaving water, pasts and present in celebration. Nor need a past be very ancient: 'QE2 SAILS IN SEARCH OF DISTANT MEMORIES' (*DM*, 23 July) was a typical headline and one strong enough to stand a little examination.

The opening paragraph read: 'The world's most famous cruise liner set sail yesterday on a historic voyage.'

The second one informed us that the occasion was the 150th anniversary of Cunard, the voyage 'a five-day cruise of the British Isles'.

Overtones and undertones must already be criss-crossing in the reader's mind. This after all is the *QE2,* launched in 1967 for a dual role in the summer transatlantic passenger trade and the winter cruise market. It is not *the Queen Elizabeth,* completed in 1940 and to this day the world's largest passenger liner, genuinely an historic vessel the memory of which, if not the actuality, is meet to be a proud part of the (British) national heritage (pity that its end, scrapped as a burnt-out wreck off Hong Kong, was so ignominious; but an original sand-blasted glass mural is preserved by Southampton City Museum).

It was, then, *the* Queen Elizabeth's Johnny-come-lately replacement that was making this 'historic voyage', all five days of it; and to, of all exotic places, the British Isles – great excitement all round, appropriate to, not the centenary or the bi-centenary of some significant national event, but to the one and a half centenary of a private shipping company. *QE2,* however, 'will anchor at some of the most significant ports in the history of Cunard', including Liverpool and Glasgow, be boarded by the Irish Prime Minister at Cobh – 'a town which has long been linked with the shipping line' – where the 'visit will also commemorate the million Irish emigrants Cunard has carried to America'. Almost predictably, 'it will return to a royal welcome in Southampton'.

At one level, one might almost say the normal level of the way things are done in Britain, this commemoration-cum-celebration had many of the ingredients of a quasi-national event: a big ship, a famous company name, business longevity, diplomacy with the Irish Republic, an American connection, and royalty; and the organisers could doubtless be proud of having put such a package together. At another level, however, the whole thing was ridiculous, anniversaryism gone mad when executed on this scale and for such a non-event. From one point of view, it spoke of a positively unhealthy calling-up of a past into the present; presumably it actually represented a major PR triumph.

The day after writing that mildly ironic, as I hoped, paragraph, I had to eat my words as the *Daily Mail* informed me that 'The *QE2* sailed home yesterday to an ecstatic welcome from hundreds of thousands of sightseers ... It was a historic moment for the liner, making her first visit to Liverpool to celebrate Cunard's 150th anniversary.' Never one to miss an opportunity to bring past military glories into the present, the paper included in the rest of its coverage details of Cunard's records during two World Wars and of *QE2*'s in 'the Falklands war'. Are these the 'distant memories' evoked the day before? Is this the purpose of yesterday's 'historic voyage', today's 'historic moment'; or are we just dealing with a domestic anniversary of a passenger line?

The military element was equally predictably totally missing from *The Guardian*'s report of the same event, a classic example not just of instant history but of heritage-on-the-hoof. A magnificent photograph spread across the top of its back page. It showed *QE2* surrounded by 'a jaunty flotilla of craft', hoving to off that magnificent mini-Manhattan skyline of Liverpool's Pier Head dominated by the Cunard building of 1917.

The occasion presumably, and the vivid reporting of it certainly, contained many of the elements of the present celebrating the past, of the past activating the present, in this case of many thousands of people. The liner's 'majestic arrival on the midday tide in the Mersey ... sent a tingle down the spine' (sense of occasion, emotion); ' "We'll never see this again" ' from a captain 'with 18 years on the river after 15 years at sea ... overwhelmed by the sight' (last chance scenario, 'Old Saltery'); thousands of people on the river banks (crowd scenes, popular interest); nostalgia within a simple, personalised, historical framework, from 4 July 1840, when 'Sam Cunard sent the wooden paddle steamer Britannia ... on the maiden mail voyage to Halifax and Boston', through the launch of a passenger service to New York in 1843, to 'the last liners to use the port ... in the 1970s as the tide of history pushed Liverpool into economic decline' (impersonal forces beyond local or individual control).

The celebration also contained visual interest with overt old-tymery, notably in the form of 'the Mersey Heritage's square rigged training schooner Zebu'. Salutes boomed out, balloons, fireworks, formalities (ceremonial); the captain of the Belfast ferry took 'his vessel back down river to give passengers a memorable cruise round the liner' (the personal touch 'midst pomp and circumstance). A celebratory lunch for Cunard pensioners was laid on at the Maritime Museum (looking after the old folks, here, by association, directly part of the heritage being simultaneously celebrated and created). Following the *QE2*, the arrival from the United States of the 'sister cargo container flagship, the giant Atlantic Conveyor' provided eloquent symbolism, particularly as 'There was no bunting for her . . .' (bathos). But an upbeat realism emerged for 'Liverpool knows its maritime future lies more with the likes of her than the elegant *QE2*' (optimistic merging of the presence of the past with a future in a less stylish world).

Alan Dunn's 650-word report was a super piece, probably not without its own consciously ironic undertones but immediately making me feel that I had completely misjudged this example of 'Then, now' at first sight. I had overlooked, for a start, the sheer pleasure that this, and doubtless other occasions on the cruise, gave to countless people; and Dunn's writing brought home the powerful emotions released by the celebration of not just a sense of pastness but of a past which was a very real present for millions of people; a past moreover which really has now gone for ever. Paradoxically, however, but in part precisely because of its power to trigger strong emotions, I still have doubts about the appropriateness of this particular anniversary for such junketings in Liverpool. That said, I can nevertheless appreciate that this occasion there now 'means' (whatever that means) much more than a formal, probably slightly stilted celebration of some national event in London. There might well be some sort of similar Liverpudlian occasion in AD 2000 to commemorate the tenth anniversary of the Cunard celebration. Commemoration breeds on commemoration as 'thens' become 'nows'.

Celebrating the past takes not only different forms but different subjects. Historic things and events have to compete with historic people, genuine and otherwise, for resources to mount the celebratory modes and for our attention to make them successful. 'Literary giants' – they have to be this, not just writers, to warrant celebration – are commonly the subject of anniversaryism or possibly just promotion, perhaps to draw attention to a new edition of their 'old' books (very attractive when out of copyright). Such figures from the past – and the same applies *par excellence* to painters and musicians – are particularly commemorable when they were, or can be, linked to a particular place, a past landscape and preferably one recognisably surviving into the present. Given the scale, nature and extent of change my generation has inflicted on the landscape, the last criterion is not always easy to meet, though the inventiveness of the modern tourist industry does not necessarily allow that to stand in its way.

Some 'past landscapes' nevertheless do survive to the extent that, with a little creative promotion perhaps, they can legitimately join in the contemporary celebration of dead artists – and, indeed, arguably less legitimately, of living ones and fictional characters too. A fellow-traveller on an Inter-City express recently, looking out east to the North Yorkshire Moors, spotted the white horse (completed on 4 November 1857) carved on their western flanks near Kilburn. 'Is that Herriot Country?' he chirpily asked.

Whole books wax helpfully and lyrically on this theme; there is, after all, *The Oxford Literary Guide to the British Isles* (1977). The opening paragraph of its Preface explains with clarity: 'There is a fascination about places associated with writers that has often prompted readers to become pilgrims; to visit a birthplace and contemplate the surroundings of an author's childhood, to see with fresh eyes places that inspired poems or books, to pay homage at a graveside or public memorial . . . but so many buildings have been demolished or replaced that it has been necessary to add the word 'gone' after the description . . . and leave the rest to the reader's imagination.'

There could well be a certain wryness, even a philosophical point, lurking behind this lament and the use of the word 'gone': has not what once was 'gone' anyway, whether or not the physical context remains? A dead artist however great cannot respond now to the stimulation of his locale then, whether or not it still looks more or less the same; we cannot relive an author's life nor react identically to the creative impulse he or she received from a place. If our seeing it makes us think we better understand the nature of that creativity, for all we know we may actually be plunging deeper into self-delusion. What we make of such a physical pilgrimage is basically down to our 'imagination' anyway, however much we the visitors, or they the preservers or promoters of the shrine, may like to think otherwise.

The Telegraph Magazine recently explored 'Puck of Pook's Hill, Sussex'; the National Trust preserves Beatrix Potter and Thomas Bewick properties; we can visit the real homes of Grieg in Bergen, Bernard Shaw in Ayot St Lawrence and Shakespeare in Stratford-upon-Avon. 'Thomas Hardy Country', peaking in its promotion in 1990 150 years after his birth is visitable in the Wessex countryside around his home, Max Gate, now conveniently situated just off the new Dorchester by-pass but most inconveniently specified in current debate as a National Trust property 'hidden' from members and the public. Elgar's landscape is delineated for the pilgrim around Malvern; less stationary is the essential ambience of the equivalent of 'Agatha Christie Country' in the luxury of the revived Orient Express.

In the contrasting gritty tweeness of Haworth lies the Parsonage home of the Brontë family (1820–61), now 'a literary museum furnished with a wealth of Brontë relics, including Patrick Brontë's bible, Charlotte's wedding bonnet, Anne's writing desk, the sofa where Emily died and an extensive collection of original manuscripts' (Pl. 17). Naturally, the village is central to the quite inevitable 'Brontë Country', a district of magnificent moorland enhanced with such artificial attractions as a Museum of Childhood ('Nostalgic collection of toys from a bygone era'), Keighley and Worth Valley Steam Railway ('Restored 5-mile line with stations ...'), and the Grave of Miss Lily Cove ('... Britain's first woman balloonist/parachutist, who died ... in 1906 when she became detached from her parachute'). Could a Brontë have put it better? Their Parsonage was the centre of a classic row in 1990: large enough for the Brontë family but too small for the hordes of Brontë devotees, should it be extended at all and, if so, by adding underground or to the rear? And in what architectural style: vernacular, classical, or post (neo?)-modern?

Should the original unfortunately not be available, reconstructions of the humble (of course) homes of such as today's most popular novelist, Catherine Cookson, can be seen in the museum at South Shields, South Tyneside (sorry, 'Catherine Cookson Country'). Her birthplace was unfortunately demolished some time before the impoverished local economic situation prompted the thought that, in both her persona and her historical fiction, the Metropolitan Borough Council possessed a marketable asset worthy of a 'Country'. So, as one of the points of interest on the eponymous Trail around that Country, you can see the site of the birthplace marked by an information panel in the shadow of a railway embankment at the side of a traffic roundabout.

At the other end of this celebratory scale as it were, Richard Nixon, while not perhaps primarily famous as a writer, followed Abraham Lincoln in a somewhat unusual public self-commemoration by reinstating the small wooden house in California where he was born and lived for his first ten years. This was in addition to the usual ex-Presidential library and museum, also located at this boyhood shrine.

All such modern manifestations of celebrating the life and works of creative men and women are in addition to the norms of putting up plaques on houses where they lived, of erecting statues of them in public places, of burying them in Westminster Abbey's Poets' Corner or equivalent, and of endlessly writing biographies about them or reviewing them in the literary press. And the list of the sorts of commemorable persons itself goes on extending: witness the celebration of the achievement of Richard Dimbleby, television commentator and personality, in the memorial to him placed in Westminster Abbey, near Poets' Corner, in autumn 1990.

Clearly there is a range here, in the form of celebration, the nature of the person celebrated and the motives of those both arranging the facility and taking advantage of it. Chaucer covered a number of the issues in the last two categories some six hundred years ago. That fact itself is part of our artistic heritage, of our perceived literary landscape in the mind as well as on the ground along 'the Pilgrims' Way'. The 'Way' is now, inevitably, the theme of a commercial heritage centre in Canterbury.

A nice little example of the commodification of the historical interest of a literary 'shrine property' is provided by the supposed original Old Curiosity Shop of Dickens's eponymous novel. The place where Little Nell died – 'Its authenticity is contested by the Dickens Fellowship ... But we're 999.99 per cent certain that this is the right shop' – was for sale during 1989–90. The asking price fell from £400,000 to £250,000 as the London property market collapsed. 'Now it's a bargain', the proprietor was reported as saying (*ES*, 16 July). 'Built in 1567, it's the oldest shop in London, with 200,000 visitors a year, and currently houses such curiosities as Dickens's egg cruet.' Dickens's great-granddaughter added another layer of value in reportedly saying 'Americans are very happy to think they've been to the real place and I've learnt to say nothing when they tell me. If people want to believe it's genuine they can.' 'Veni, vidi the cruet, ergo credo', with apologies to another literary giant and fighting man, would seem to sum up this all too familial homespun assessment of customer need. And it may be accurate.

An Alabaman lady said more or less exactly the same to me a few years ago. She, together with the rest of her packaged, grey-haired companions, had listened as they chanced on me explaining to a television camera, high on the cliffs of 'Arthurian-steeped Tintagel' in Cornwall, that recent research cast grave doubts on whether the site had anything to do with King Arthur, even if he existed, and that in any case the ruined buildings on the site were not those of a Celtic monastery in the fifth/sixth centuries AD. Speaking impromptu to the camera in her turn, she gave me the great put-down with considerable cogency: 'We have listened to the professor with interest and no doubt what he says is factually correct; but we have come three thousand miles to see this beautiful place and share in your wonderful history. I believe in King Arthur and I want to believe that I've walked where he walked. We've nothing like this where I come from and nothing the professor says is going to stop me taking away the memories I came for.' So off she and her companions quested, happy in their unshaken pasts, their pleasure unalloyed by an historicity they neither sought nor despised but did not need.

Personal belief is a powerful medium for bringing the past forward into the present. In its institutional form as religion, it tends towards the conservative; personal belief, though often inspired by hope for a post-mortem future, is also almost by definition rooted in a past. Both draw on pasts compounded of events, lives of holy predecessors, beliefs, writings, places, pig-headedness and defiance of reason, a whole cultural package to be revered and activated in the present. Celebrating present beliefs and future hopes inevitably becomes mixed up with celebrating various pasts especially at the great shrine sites, usually themselves of considerable age in their venerability and often in their buildings too. Whether events believed to have occurred at such sites actually happened in an historically verifiable form seems almost to be beside the point when their powerful symbolism evokes such devotion. Nevertheless, here is another of those cases of parallel pasts. The one is historical, the other is believed in whether or not it is factually valid but is now in any case 'historical' in the sense that the belief has itself existed for a long time.

Quite inevitably, the pastness of religion carries through into ordinary daily life, even in secular society. In Britain, for example, a long-running current affair concerns the celebration of the Sabbath, the religious day of rest decreed by the Established Church, and therefore itself a tradition, for long buttressed by legislation. A popular columnist, Keith Waterhouse (*DM, 23 April*), went straight to the heart of the matter with ironic percipience: 'The Silly Sunday is part of Britain's heritage. Knowing that we can buy cooked sausages on the Sabbath, but not uncooked sausages ... should give us all a glow of pride.' His remark incidentally incorporates a somewhat unfashionable assumption that our national heritage is first and foremost a matter of pride. The tenor of government and the heritage industry in recent years has rather been to the effect that it is primarily something which at the very least ought to be a nice little earner.

Waterhouse, however, immediately returns to the party line (parentheses this author's). 'The Silly Sunday (presumably as part of our heritage?) is good for the tourist trade ... and it is good for the family' (very much a 'Victorian value' concept in recent official adumbration). The punch line is 'We would become the only Christian country in the world to close down churches on Sunday.'

An irony is of course that many churches have already been closed down, for all the days of the week and for ever. Hence the double ambiguity of the name of that most worthy of all preservation bodies, The Friends of Friendless Churches. Claims are now being made that congregations are increasing again, that some churches will need to be enlarged, and that the last thing the Established Churches should be doing is disposing of their building assets. Nevertheless, ex-religious buildings are now big business. In the conservation world, much effort goes into identifying and supporting those worth keeping: 427 grant applications were made to

English Heritage in 1988–9, and £7.1 million offered in grant. That's a great deal of work for many people. Finding alternative uses compatible with their original function and continued physical existence is also difficult; one solution is for Christian places of worship to continue their function but for another religion. Down the road from my house, a synagogue was turned into would-be chi-chi boutiques and a coffee shop; long before it was burnt down, images of Christ in the Temple accompanied my every bun. In the property market the sites of such buildings are often valuable in redevelopment terms. Furthermore, the buildings themselves can provide challenging opportunities to make desirable residences that are different. They provide a way of celebrating self as well as pastness.

A converted Methodist chapel on the outskirts of a Pennine village either can make a nice home or its space can be conveniently adapted for sympathetic secular business, for example as art gallery, craft shoppe or old tyme tea rooms. To choose that spray of dried flowers you did not realise you needed, or spread your homemade scone with organic strawberry jam where not long ago lay preachers thundered out their weekly message of unscripted inspiration on Eternal Truths, is an attractive contrast to the mindless commercial transactions of depersonalised supermarket check-outs. Such experiences are indeed a form of celebration, of the present's capacity for sensible conversion of the past, especially by playing on personalisation in exactly the same way as the ad-men try to make us believe each of us can stand out from the crowd by acquiring their product. To be dressed by Ralph Lauren is, so they would have us believe, to celebrate a lot.

A day in the life of the past   5

To look at the presence of the past on just one day is to sympathise with Charles Dickens's Mr Grewgious: 'it's like looking down the throat of Old Time' (*Edwin Drood*, Chapter 9). Old Time, sometimes dressed up as Olde Tyme, dances with contemporary life; even in death. 'The funeral industry yesterday laid to rest its heritage of spasmodic preparation for eternal farewells ...' (*G*, 3 July). Doubtless the reporter was consciously using the word 'heritage' here with tongue characteristically in cheek. All the same, the concept of even this service industry having its own heritage illustrates a characteristic ubiquity and ambivalence of the past among us today.

The 8th of July 1990 was a typical English summer Sunday. The south of the country enjoyed sunshine, much of the north was under cloud; both were windy. It happened to be the day on which I sat down to write this chapter; the date is of no greater significance, as I now know to be the case, for any one can play this game on any day. Yet, perhaps unfortunately for my thesis, it was quite an exceptional day in its way, as much of the population organised its Sabbath around the televisual opportunities of the final of the men's singles at Wimbledon in the afternoon and the final of the Association Football World Cup in Rome in the evening.

Naturally, the tons of newsprint issued by the Sunday press reflected these major sporting interests to come, while reporting on the Saturday's major events, such as Finals day at Henley and England's gloriously typical fourth place in the football World Cup. There was also comment on the continuing reverberations of the political changes on the world scene and particularly in eastern Europe, notably the NATO meeting in London during the week and the gathering that weekend of the leaders of the world's seven richest industrial nations at Houston, Texas. Yet, despite all these major preoccupations with the present and the future, the same newspapers also typically gushed with the past. The fact that there was so much competition for newsprint space in its way emphasised my point. Take any single day, and there is an awful lot of past in public; this is just a selection to illustrate some of its appearances and their ramifications on one particular day.

'Fishing for tackle of a vintage era' was the headline for 'Showcase' on the 'Personal Finance' page of the *Sunday Times*. It was flanked to the right by a photograph of a 'cast replica of the British record salmon, of 64lb, caught by Miss Georgina Ballantine in 1922', and the list of Britain's Top 100 shares. Their prices and those of bits of somewhat arcane equipment appeared as equals in a commodified present. Though the paper's thinking reader might nevertheless have pondered momentarily over the implications of an image of a past presented as a photograph of a replica of a fish caught sixty-eight years previously.

No doubt there have been specialist collectors of fishing tackle for their historical interest for many years; there is indeed a museum of such at Alnwick, Northumberland. It is on the premises of the renowned Hardy Bros, makers since 1872 of precisely the sort of tackle recommended in 1990 to its readers by a major Sunday newspaper as worthy of their attention, primarily for financial reasons. 'Prices are rising. Two Hardy Perfect reels were sold in 1984 at £380 and £480. Today they would sell for £1,200–£1,500 each ... Prices are even higher in America ... There has also been a big rise in the price of fish trophies, those stuffed fish that look so good on the study wall ...'

'*Research for Fishing Tackle, A Collector's Guide* meant delving into nineteenth-century trade directories and archives at London's Guildhall, the London Museum and Kew Palace ... The book includes a comprehensive price guide to the reels, rods and tackle that have been sold in Britain and America in the past six years.' In contemporary Britain it is surprising neither that the cost of such vital financial information is £35 nor that it is obtainable from an auctioneer's house.

This particular item played across part of the range of the past in contemporary life. The subject was basically a fairly obscure field of expertise, items from which have been lovingly collected by a small number of people from the vast army of enthusiasts who follow, in many cases practise, Britain's most popular sport, fishing. During the 1980s, however, such tackle became financially collectable as admiration for its combination of 'technical innovation ... matched by the beauty of hand craftsmanship' was converted into rising investment value. Now, the attractiveness of this field to the market was drawn to the attention of its readers by one of the 'quality Sundays'. It baited its hook, so to speak, by mentioning the appeal of items in this field to the fogey mentality ('stuffed fish which look so good on the study wall'), by lightly scoring the authentic historicity ('archives at London's Guildhall') of this historic byway, and by making access to it as easy as possible through detailing the information now available in this field to the potential investor with no real knowledge, nor probably genuine interest, in it. Much the same has happened in many other fields of 'collectables' (see Chapter 9).

Central to the first page of the Appointments section in the same prestigious 'Sunday' was an image presumably immediately recognisable by all readers: Stonehenge. The familiar silhouette, viewed from inside the stone circle looking north-east out through the lintelled trilithons, was highlighted by a light-source beyond the central uprights; yet somehow the rays radiating symmetrically from it cut across the nearer, viewer's side of the great sarsens. Never mind, the image is the name of the game, so the writer of the large-print words on what is predictably an advertisement was able to assume that the reader had not only recognised this particular image but had also given it a meaning.

'Today's IT systems are somewhat more complex ...' said the advert, immediately implying it is common knowledge that Stonehenge was a computer. 'Umps' as Mr Grewgious said on another occasion (Chapter 11). Never mind: we get the message that the stones represent a relatively unsophisticated way of handling information. The text was quite explicit on the matter: 'Stonehenge ranks as one of the first computer systems ever built.' As a statement of fact, this should be referred to the Advertising Standards Authority, for there is not a shred of indisputable evidence that Stonehenge was ever either designed or used as a computer; to think otherwise is to fall victim to contemporary relativism in interpretation. Yet the interest of the advertisement lay not in its archaeological accuracy but in its use of image and assumptions, as much about its audience in the late twentieth century AD as its subject in the twentieth century BC.

'Softlab' was here in this example also advertising jobs for those 'with at least 2 years' product marketing experience' at salaries high in the professorial range achieved by the few after twenty and more years at the academic quarry-face. The company clearly saw a use for hard-core archaeology in promoting its software.

The deeply-embedded and continuing value of the Stonehenge image was further illustrated on the same day by *The Mail on Sunday*. Its photograph showed a somewhat ragged version of the familiar profile, but this time created by scrap cars stood on end. Three trilithons were formed by a vehicle across the top of each of three pairs of 'uprights' in a temporary structure erected as part of the set for a television series (broadcast six months later, January 1991). Again, the image, however sketchy, was all, for by its very nature this structure, unlike the original, was put up with an intended life-span of days rather than centuries.

The caption was revealing: 'On a misty Suffolk marsh [mysterious note without which no Stonehenge item would be complete], a familiar outline thrusts towards the sky [old but dynamic] . . . Stonehenge? No, Carhenge! Far from the real ancient edifice on Salisbury Plain [compulsory nod towards authenticity], engineers and inventors [OK chaps] Tim Hunkin and Rex Garrod [suitably macho names] have built their own monument [transference of the virtues of the original to the new] to a modern idol [implying a present-day function of the original]. The striking structure [is it really? – only by association], made from rusting vehicles . . . is for their Channel 4 series "The Secret Life of . . ." . . . which describes how everyday objects work [plant of expectation factor: are we to be told how cars, Stonehenge or carhenges work?]. In the last series, they built a pyramid [playing to the other of the two most familiar images from antiquity, see Chapter 11] of washing machines [one of the most familiar icons of the consumer society] and now hope Carhenge will achieve the same visual impact. Rex said: "Because the motor car has become a religion [he said it!], we chose this [i.e. Stonehenge, therefore taking a religious function of Stonehenge for granted] to illustrate a programme on it" i.e. the motor car. He thereby drew a most stimulating parallel between an artefact of natural materials, ancient, unique, mysterious, permanent and static, and an artefact of processed materials, contemporary, mass-produced, common-or-garden, transitory and mobile.'

Apparently unexhausted by that *tour de force*, Rex reportedly concluded: 'Conservationists can stop worrying, too. Carhenge won't last anywhere as long as the original . . .' A bit of an anti-climax, that, with its cliché implication that conservationists are worrying fogeys, despite the apparent *non sequitur*; on the other hand, to judge by the photograph, the shorter the existence of this tatty simulation of one of the world's great structures, the better.

Incidentally, but as a matter of fact, this Suffolk pseudo-replica was not as original in conception, and certainly not as sophisticated in execution, as the paper might suggest. Of five Stonehenge simulacra already in existence, two made of old cars have already been built in North America. One, the Autohenge (1986), is near Lake Ontario, the other, the Carhenge (1987), is in Nebraska. Both were also erected for temporary purposes but each still stands, the former preserved already as a place of solstice ritual and rock (what else?) music, the latter as officially-approved sculpture.

Another long-running image also featured hugely in the same *Mail on*

Sunday. 'The Queen Mother at 90; What a Wonderful Life', 'A Cele-bration in Words and Pictures' occupied the whole of a supplement to its *You Magazine.* It is no secret that the English, perhaps even the British, are obsessed by their Royal family (Pl. 18); or at least, the British press is. So it was no surprise, on this or any other Sunday, to find a 'Royal' featured, nor is it entirely unknown for the *whole* of a magazine, as in this case, to be devoted to 'The Queen Mum' (to quote its pally famili-arity). The interest and relevance here, in a classic example of anni-versaryism, was that the treatment was entirely backward-looking. It started 'at the close of the great Victorian era' with Her Majesty's 'gentle Edwardian childhood' (actually a nice and finely-judged periodisation since Elizabeth Angela Marguerite Bowes-Lyon was born just six months before Queen Victoria's death). And curiously, apart from an otherwise undated 1990 photograph of the QM with a jockey, the latest picture was of Her Majesty on 4 August 1989, her 89th birthday; and understandably, nothing was said of the future except for the back page's impersonal exit line: '. . . and the dynasty goes on'.

A similar note was struck in a similar feature on the same day in the *Sunday Times*'s *Style and Travel* section. 'Everlasting Rose' was the headline to an article about the USA's nearest equivalent to the British Royal family: 'America's most famous family will gather . . . to celebrate the 100th birthday of a living legend . . . Rose Kennedy . . . America's most famous *Mom.*' Familial longevity, Western society's preconceptions of maternalism, pedestal-occupancy, and an assumed familiarity, rather than Royalty as such, would seem to be important elements in this contemporary version of ancestor-worship through the old but still living.

While Associated Newspapers might be thought to have opportunistically jumped the gun, possibly even for commercial reasons, by publishing their QM supplement a month before Her Majesty's actual birthday, it would seem only fair to remark that London's rush-hour traffic was blocked by an even earlier processional celebration along The Mall on 27 June. Schoolchildren danced on Horse Guards Parade dressed as Teddy Bears (another powerful 'heritage' symbol with Royal undertones) and the massed bands of the Household Brigade, the Royal Marines and the RAF blew their appropriate musical kisses.

The anniversary proved to be an extended occasion. The rest of 1990 used this 90th birthday to feature a remarkable lady many times. And fittingly so, many would argue, doubtless echoing a people fed by its media as besotted in particular by its Royal past. The usual commercial note was nevertheless struck here too: in the autumn, 'To celebrate the Queen Mother's 90th Year', loyal and discerning citizens with an eye to investment enhancement were offered 'An exclusive, tasteful selection of commemorative pieces of fine bone china and crystal', in Limited Editions of course, 'essential to the serious collector of Royal memorabilia'.

A family renowned for its dedication to public duty and dogs may seem to have little in common with that undeniable musical genius, Mozart; except possibly Middle European roots. Yet competing with the Queen Mother in the anniversary stakes on 8 July was the *Sunday Times Magazine*'s relatively upmarket 'Mozart World'. 'A major celebration begins today', we were told, as we were enjoined to 'Start collecting our special stickers for this week's free wallchart'. And it transpired that 'begins' was the key word, for the treatment this Sunday merely trailed 'other events leading up to our major autumn festival of music in honour of Mozart', 'the world's best-loved composer'. So clearly *Sunday Times Magazine* readers were going to be firmly stuck in, or at least exposed to, the eighteenth century for some months to come (as indeed proved to be the case). And not only *Sunday Times* readers: by the last weekend of the year even *The Guardian* was already exhibiting signs of Mozartian *ennui*, yet *the actual bicentennial had not even begun.*

Not that that had deterred the *Sunday Times* itself on 8 July. In a classic example of a flying start, the newspaper, as distinct from the *Magazine,* emphasised the commitment of its publishing house to the past in the future by plunging into its own 'celebration of genius' of a man from the past 'in advance of the bicentenary of Mozart's death in 1791'. Clearly, you cannot afford to be slow off the mark in the anniversary stakes these days. Pre-anniversaryism is a great marketing concept: we should all prepare to celebrate the millennium in 1997 for heritage, like Christmas, comes earlier every year.

Without in any way implying that the *Sunday Times Magazine* is more prone to pastness than similar products, merely by looking at it a little more closely than the normal matitudinal skim really brought home the extent to which a range of pasts imbues the present; at least as represented by an up-market, market-oriented, right-of-centre weekly publication. The advertisements characteristically played to the past. The double-page spread extolling a particularly classy car, for example, drew attention to its 'legendary' engine and, evoking a bygone age of trusty craft-folk, the 'hand-crafted elegance' and 'hand-stitched tweeds' of its interior. Another interior, again 'Individually crafted and installed', claimed to give you a 'Home Study' ... designed to blend with original architectural features'. Rather puzzlingly, however, it seemed to consist entirely of late-1980s populist repro. Seemingly similar, though definitely up-market in its come-on glitz as illustrated in the colour plate, was the beautiful bogusness inviting readers to a weekend in 'Edwardian Hotels', naturally replete with that great, anachronistic tradition, 'a full English breakfast'.

A particular Swiss watch, like the 'Classic Furniture' in another advert, was associated with a nineteenth-century date (1860) to invoke, presumably, an image of reliability additional to the prestige and quality implied by its Swissness. Equally firmly rooted in the implied solidity of that virtuous period was the predictable advertisement for 'The Original Victorian Conservatories'. Their price range of £5,000–£50,000 fairly precisely defined the magazine's target audience. Inching back through the nineteenth century, a hotel chain promoted one of its establishments as *'built in Greek Revival style, c. 1836 by John Pinch the Younger for General Augustus Andrews'*. Clever writing, that, nicely circumventing the awkwardness of that 1836 date which is not quite 'Victorian' yet too late for 'Georgian'. By boldly quoting the slightly exotic names of two very minor worthies, at one and the same time the text gave just that touch of authenticity while conveying the hint of an implication that the reader *ought* to know who they were.

If you took the hint, you could well be on the way to succumbing to the temptation to 'save £70' by enrolling as a member of the Ancient and Medieval History Book Club in order to acquire for £5 instead of £75 three volumes of *The Oxford History of England*. Expectation that reading your selected purchases, as implied by the advertisement, will be 'exciting' might possibly fail to be realised should you choose, for example, Mackie's *The Earlier Tudors 1485–1558*.

Gliding by four pages featuring the creation of a snack being marketed under the top-hatted, redolent-of-the-past logo of 'Phileas Fogg', the avid reader could then have marvelled at a full-page advertisement for 'An extraordinary Scale Classic Built by Hand [again!] with 144 Components'. The model in question was 'An authentic replica of the famed Phantom I ... fully authorized by Rolls-Royce Motor Cars Ltd'. This also had a 'legendary' engine but one wondered whether such was already the case 'when the original Cabriolet went for an outing in 1929'. Perhaps it did not cost much more then than, at £95, its 1:24 scale replica in 1990.

This rampant nostalgia was not, however, signposted as such whereas a major feature article, 'Preaching to the Converted', was unambiguously labelled 'Heritage' and thickly underlined in red. So we knew where we were.

We were being told of the judgements of the Country House Awards, a scheme by the newspaper and an estate agent 'designed to find the best recent conversion of a non-residential building into a country home'. Highly commendable, of course, and very much *à la mode au fin du siècle*: Establishment sponsorship of something usefully combining conservation, conversion, domesticity and, probably, shrewd investment.

One could fairly confidently predict the types of building which would be among the winners: a Victorian industrial building, a redundant church, a barn, a folly of some sort, a garden building and a mill. The winners were a Victorian water tower, a redundant church, an Essex barn, a circular almshouse, the site of a former garden glass-house and a Welsh water mill.

One could only infer what historical and archaeological damage may have been inadvertently perpetrated on the structures and other evidence above and below ground in these well-intentioned and imaginative projects. Only in the case of the church did the write-up specify that 'archaeological investigation was made a condition of planning permission' (Pl. 19). It almost threw away the extremely interesting academic information that, as a result, a Roman cemetery and a Saxon church were shown to have occupied the site before the present building. The difference between real archaeological interest, the stuff of which basic history is made, and things past as a quite interesting consumable could hardly have been more pointed – or so one might have thought; but the piece ground on with unconscious ambivalence. For owner and architect, we were told, 'there were tangible rewards *too*' (this author's italics). 'When the wooden floor of the nave was taken up, the original York stone pavement was found.' Was one wrong in thinking that the implication of this remark, made apparently within the assumed priority of a materialistic frame of reference, was that the 'reward' lay, not in the originality or scientific interest of the pavement but in its value in consisting of currently valuable *York* stone?

On that same day woods were also under threat as modern society, this time as represented by the *Observer Magazine* and a planning application for a single house, pursued its ceaseless attack on its environment. This time it was natural as well as historical. 'Domesday for historic woodland?' asked the headline. The particular example concerned Sydenham Hill Woods, 'the nearest ancient woodland to central London ... just a couple of leagues from St Paul's Cathedral' (who on earth these days knows the length of a 'league'? – but it's a good archaic term to flavour the article appropriately) ... 'one of the few remaining fronds of the Great North Wood ...' (distant resonances of Toad and Ratty?). In addition to the usual rare mosses and fungi, flat-footed flies and yellow archangels that tend to inhabit such places, 'These woods of oak and hornbeam were FIRST MENTIONED IN THE DOMESDAY BOOK' (the capitals are this author's to emphasise the tone of awe he perhaps wrongly detected in the phrase). And they really were historical because John Evelyn was mugged there in 1652 and Pissarro painted the view from the footbridge over the now defunct railway.

An association of art and industrial archaeology seems an appropriately high note on which to end this day in the life of the past, as witnessed selectively in three Sunday papers alone. And the travel articles and advertisements, many hawking numerous pasts, have not even been mentioned. 'Look on my works, ye Mighty, and despair'; shudder at the thought of how long this chapter could have been.

6 | *Days-out in the past*

The past plays both a general and a very specific part in leisure activities, especially holidaying. The media certainly seem to think that and visitor figures at heritage attractions give substance to the hype.

Some 70 million visits were made to historic properties in 1989, nearly half of them to cathedrals and churches, and some 59 million admissions were additionally counted at museums and galleries. Beyond such official figures are countless millions of visits to other available bits of pastness, for example at many attractions not included in the official returns and to historic town centres, rural sites and landscapes where access is free and uncountable. Nor is it totally unknown for people to visit official heritage sites after hours and therefore not be counted. Even so, some of the statistics are indicative of contemporary sociology rather than just past interest. The 1987 General Household Survey, for example, found that 8 per cent of adults in Britain had visited an historic building in the month before the interviews, that percentage rising to 10 per cent among those aged 30–44 and to 14 per cent among professional people. A Time Use Survey in 1989 pointed to an average among its sample population of over five visits per quarter to historic buildings, museums and galleries, an amazing figure implying some twenty such visits per person per year. The proportion of people visiting historic buildings varied from 22 per cent in the fourth quarter (October–December) to 40 per cent in the third (July–September).

An annual problem in that third quarter is what to do with the kids during the school holiday. Part of the solution was in *The Observer*'s *School's Out* supplement of 22 July, the Sunday of the weekend immediately after the end of the state school summer term. The Sunday papers reported consequential day-long traffic jams in southern English temperatures of 90°F (33°C). Where were they trying to go, all these happy, sweltering families in immobile tin boxes? *The Observer* indicated the sort of destination they should have had in mind, not least by offering

'Discount vouchers for dozens of days out' on its outside front cover. The dose was repeated on successive Sundays, as it is every holiday time in many newspapers, so this is only a sample of one example.

While the jolly descriptive list of places to go to included theme parks, nature reserves and adventure centres, the past enjoyed a fairly prominent place in the presumably careful choice of what was intended to be an enjoyable holiday with, possibly even for, children. In fact the blurb covertly stated that the Offers 'are designed to tell you about some of the best day out locations in the country and save you money *while you are having fun*' (this author's italics). The first instalment of a weekly listing meeting those criteria was quite interesting in itself.

Of thirty-three places, twelve were straight-down-the-line major archaeological/historical sites of at least national importance. Whatever may be done or not done in the way of presenting them to visitors, these are among the real jewels in terms of man-made heritage. At Rievaulx, North Yorkshire, for example, the ruins are those of a genuine abbey of considerable academic significance architecturally where real Cistercian monks pursued their lives of devotion during some four hundred years until just over four hundred years ago. It was one of the four sites listed that are now in the care of English Heritage (below p. 88). The other three were Westminster Abbey Chapter House ('One of the great treasure troves of London . . . the Abbey Museum contains medieval royal effigies'), Dover Castle, Kent ('. . . Roman lighthouse, Saxon church, Norman keep and underground tunnels . . . Voucher does not include Hellfire Corner'), and Stonehenge ('Britain's most extraordinary prehistoric monument and . . . mecca for the nation's pagans'). Queen's House, Greenwich ('One of the few surviving examples of the innovative work of Inigo Jones, the man who revolutionised English architecture in the 17th century'), is also part of the official state heritage but is managed under a different aegis.

Four of the other 'real' heritage sites are properties in the care of the National Trust (below p. 92). One, Wallington, Northumberland, is a fine country house with grounds conforming to popular perceptions of what the Trust preserves; the other three perhaps conformed less readily to preconceptions about Trust properties, because of either their nature or their location. Speke Hall, Liverpool ('Half-timbered . . . with marvellous homely rooms'), tries to retain its historic integrity in adverse circumstances, in practice in the middle of a vast airfield (the comings and goings of which might well be of more interest to the recalcitrant child than the 'homely rooms', however 'marvellous'). Moseley Old Hall ('Elizabethan house with secret room which saved the life of Charles II . . . knot garden'), four miles north of Wolverhampton, lies in an area not necessarily first choice for holidaying *Observer* families; but Dolaucothi Gold Mines are in the right sort of area, south-west Wales, and have an address, Pumsaint, Llanwrda, Dyfed, enticing in its slightly mysterious unpronounceability to Anglo-Saxon tongues. Furthermore, while children may not exactly be turned on by the prospect of a setting 'amid wooded hillsides overlooking the Cothi valley', even some of them might possibly accede to a family day out garnished by a 'Miners' Way Trail with opencast sites and tunnels and ... pick marks left in the rocks by slaves working for their Roman masters'. While that interpretation may be a bit dodgy in purist eyes, the setting and the underground tour (even if it costs an extra £3 per adult and £1.75 per child, NT members half price) offer an element of exploration and adventure regardless of any personal historical vibes or interpretive absolutes.

Subterraneity rather than historicity was more overtly the come-on at Wookey Hole Caves and Mill, Wells. This is the first example from the *Observer* list of the big alternative to what can be loosely identified as the quasi-official and thoroughly professional heritage (see below p. 87). The Caves and Mill belong to the commercial company which runs Madame Tussaud's, so essentially this heritage attraction at and in the southern foot of the Mendip Hills is in being as a business. This need not matter to the family enjoying its holiday – provided enjoyment *is* coming its way – and the *Observer* does not explain the point whereas, interestingly for the implications (of high quality? of boringness?), it identified sites run by English Heritage and The National Trust.

Wookey Caves, which are indeed visually spectacular by any standards, are properly presented mainly as a natural phenomenon, though they contain considerable archaeological significance too, 'on a half-mile tour through well-lit caverns as [visitors] follow the underground route of the mysterious River Axe carved out over 250,000 years'. History-cum-industrial-archaeology comes as a relatively recent addition at the end of the tour, incorporating 'Britain's last working handmade paper mill and an Edwardian Penny Pier, complete with brass band and vintage machines which children can spend hours playing using real old pennies'. A further attraction in the near future will presumably be vintage machines using real old 5p coins (deceased 1990 and a fair candidate, following the honest shilling, for instant numismatic nostalgia). Pity about the Edwardiana really, irrelevant and somewhat demeaning as they are to the genuine awesomeness of the Caves, but business is business, the building was standing there doing nothing and the owners needed to put some of their spare junk somewhere. In a sense the solution is brilliant, given the eclectic paradigm of the heritage business, adding doubtless welcome novelty to the family visit and a sense of value for the £12.35 entrance fee.

Equally magnificent in its way and as authentic at core is Littlecote Park in Berkshire, another *Observer* recommendation; but it was even more expensive for the family (entrance £14.50, but only up to two children, which would hit many *Observer*-reading families). Essentially, and again of considerable academic interest, what is on offer is a '100-acre park and magnificent Tudor manor house where the largest remaining collection of Civil War armour is hung in the Great Hall'. To that has been added a 'Farmyard with traditional breeds of pig, sheep, cattle and poultry, medicinal and culinary herb, rose and traditional knot gardens. Plus steam railway, giant adventure playground, regular jousting tournaments and falconry displays. In the grounds is one of the most exciting [above p. 37] Roman excavations in Great Britain'. The Roman site, containing an important temple and Orpheic mosaic and incidentally overlain by a medieval settlement crucial to understanding the local landscape history, is genuine enough (though the mosaic was over-restored) and so was its professional investigation, though it was a novel move to start the latter a decade ago as entertainment. The house chapel and armour are historically important too. Much of the rest, however, was 'created heritage', not necessarily incorrect in its replication but of no authenticity whatsoever in its antiquity since it dates from the 1980s. In that it is now redundant, following a change in the proposed use of the house and grounds, presumably it will be discarded; but one wonders whether Littlecote as it was in mid-1990 is not somehow as representative of its decade, and therefore as 'archaeologically significant' as is, say, a Roman villa site which we go to some lengths to preserve.

Whether any of this matters intellectually, educationally, on the family day out is debatable but probably not in terms of direct, superficial holiday-type enjoyment. Certainly the wide range of historically-based experiences at Littlecote helped explain, and would doubtless seek to justify, the entrance fee; and doubtless too that range offers an attraction to the family seeking to occupy the children which would not be perceived as being available were the house and grounds to be presented alone for their own intrinsic historical interest and aesthetic pleasure-giving potential. The needs of familial palatability require a penumbral floss. In a sense, then, family-based participation in the authentic past, so essential for financial reasons, is actually inimical to the spirit of that authenticity.

The final authentic site in the *Observer* list was the odd one out. Denbigh Castle and Town Wall, Clwyd, are not so much a 'dead' monument given new life as an attraction for tourists to visit, as with the previous examples; rather is Denbigh a living town which, like so many historic urban centres, contains within it various pieces of historic structure surviving from, and witness to, the fact of its urban nature. The castle, built like many others in north Wales by Edward I during his subjugation of the area, is the town's centrepiece, with walls surrounding the town that grew up because of the castle. The whole forms an impressive set of medieval militarism, characteristically softened by the ecclesiastical buildings of a friary, a church and a chapel. Not much hype there, nor any theme-parkery to provide non-historical entertainment or divert attention from the authenticity which is what Denbigh is all about. Whether, while there, the grown-ups pause to ponder upon the symbolism implicit in the place, and possibly share their thoughts with their children, about wider and continuing issues of conquest, imperialism and the rights of small nations and ethnic minorities, is probably unlikely in the present context of the family day out; but to mention the thought is to touch on matters fundamental to heritage considerations.

Nevertheless, they lurked just beneath the surface of three other attractions in the list which also use the past as part of their attractiveness. At Standalone Farm, Letchworth, Hertfordshire, the past element is minor – 'a working blacksmith's shop' – where the main attraction is a working farm at which 'children can watch staff milking cows or feeding the pigs'. Is this an outstanding example of creating a tourist diversion as part of agricultural 'diversification' without actually doing anything different? Whitbread Hop Farm, Paddock Wood, Kent, also 'works', as it has done since the sixteenth century, but it is a long way further down the road of conscious heritagism. It 'has a fine collections [*sic*] of Victorian oast houses' (noticeable how 'Victorian', that former word of bad taste and dullness in the recent past, has during the 1980s acquired a sturdy ring of worthy respectability and reasonable antiquity). Worthiness is doubtless the hallmark of the 'cowlmaker, cartwright, cricket-ball manufacturer, farrier, potter, and several other interesting local craftsmen plus a selection of ducks, cows, goats, sheep, pigs, and rabbits' – a classic example of the enhancement of the mundane by journalese. 'Plus hop museum with video show, mannequins in period costume and a variety of tools of the trade' (mannequins of whom? of what? in which period? which trade? does it matter?).

But does this apotheosis of rural culture also address questions of agricultural labourers' wages and living conditions, about the exploitation of people in the hop fields in particular? In its silence on such matters, the brief *Observer* description may well be giving a false picture of rustic idyllism gone beserk; but, on the other hand, a reader with a sense of historical balance could become a little anxious at the thought of all those families with their *Observer* vouchers letting one child in free with each paying adult if *all* they received in the way of farming history was *only* imaged around skilled and satisfied rustics loyally serving a munificent landowner.

At least the last site on the list to be mentioned here was honest in its blurb. Watermouth Castle, near Ilfracombe, Devon, is an 'Elegant 19th-century castle full of nostalgic bygones including gramophones, a crystal set and a ration book'. The owners may possibly have suspected that the number of families willing to drive a long way to see an actual ration book might be somewhat circumscribed (and after all, although belonging to the mists of antiquity, i.e. I had one, a ration book is not, strictly speaking, even Victorian). Anyway, as mothers will be glad to note, for they make the decisions about family trip destinations, Watermouth Castle also boasts 'crafts, Haunted mill, miniature steam carousel and tubeslide'.

The familiar recipe for concocting 'dayout heritage' is again apparent: first catch your history (old house, castle, etc.), chuck in a bit of pastness (jousts, bygones, etc.) with whatever else is to hand (crafts, tubeslide, etc.), stir to remove integrity and allow eclecticism to surface, and then simmer until tacky, with froth on top.

So much for formal or organised visits to sites on the market to cater for visitor interest. There are lots of other sorts of sites, and indeed all sorts of other ways of experiencing the past. The variety in what people do at sites is actually extremely wide and, sometimes, distinctly odd.

You may wish to enjoy a brush with the heritage police at Stonehenge on 21 June or 21 December but most people seek other ways of enjoying the past about them; not always, it must be said, to the benefit of the monuments, whatever the motives of the visitor on his or her day out. While Stonehenge is protected all the time, many other prehistoric stone circles, burial mounds and other structures elsewhere are not, and yet they seem to suffer little harm perhaps because they offer places for quiet contemplation. Curiously, damage to these can occur by additions as well as depletions. Bronze Age cairns at one viewpoint on the Brecon Beacons, for example, have been severely reduced, stone by stone, at the hands of thousands of climbers; probably few realised the heaps of stone were anything other than natural, but then should they not have been respecting that sort of heritage too?

Heritage stone tends to travel further when visitors can arrive by vehicle: limestone blocks from prehistoric and Roman structures in the Yorkshire Dales, for example, have contributed significantly to many a surburban rockery. Lots of prehistoric cairns in upland areas have been hollowed out to make children's 'castles', animal shelters or shooting butts. Others have been topped up to make them, in modern eyes, a more prominent landscape feature (Pl. 20).

Presumably most of this is unconscious archaeological damage, sub-limating a similar urge to that which leads fathers and children on a day out to block up or divert a moorland stream. It is a matter of helping Nature, not man, to get it right. On the other hand, some incidents are quite certainly deliberate and a matter of helping Man, not Nature, to get it right. The date of that enigmatic chalk-cut figure on the Sussex Downs, the Long Man of Wilmington, may continue to be debatable but its authenticity, antiquity and merit as a remarkable work of art are not; yet it was only 'pranksters' who painted a smile on to his face (*DM*, 18 August). It is typical of the popular press to use such a jovial word for vandals. Would it be merely a 'prank' to wipe the smile off the original Mona Lisa? But then the National Trust allowed for TV purposes a whitewash cloak to be draped over the left arm of the Cerne Giant; some would doubtless have wished it draped elsewhere. Where indeed does one draw the lines at the monument? – through them, would be the reply of the leyliners, another group frequently spending good days at the monuments.

Archaeological sites are also sources for the collector. Removing anything from Scheduled Sites is illegal but that does not prevent treasure-hunting taking place. Roman and medieval sites are the prime targets since they existed in times which produced metal artefacts, notably coins. The activities here range from well-organised, nocturnal plunder using metal-detectors to the casual turf-lifting by perhaps a family on a day out. Certainly the little pock-marks of the metal detector-user in the turf have sadly become an all-too-familiar sight at British archaeological monuments over the last decade. Apart from the visual disfigurement, the damage being done out of sight underground, and to scholarship in terms of understanding, can only be guessed at, but it is undoubtedly significant whatever the motives of those so indulging themselves. Knocking off bits of vitrified fort rampart as souvenirs, as at Carradale Point, is regrettable but comparatively insignificant (Pl. 20).

The modern camera has provided people with another, archaeologically more acceptable, form of souvenir: taking photographs rather than bits of a site is much preferable. Personal snapshots apart, an important function of ancient monuments is now in meeting the needs of professional film-makers and photographers. This writer alone has 'consumed' many an ancient site in taking thousands of photographs for lecturing purposes and in making dozens of radio and television programmes over the last twenty years. It is now not at all unusual to bump into – or be shouted at by – a film or TV crew going about their business at a monument. Furthermore, all those glowing, soft-focus olde worlde illustrations in the myriad heritage books and tourist pamphlets have to be taken somewhere and nowadays other visitors will often come across photographer and camera at the ready waiting for the right combination of light, clouds and stones to capture the essence of the place. While my photographer-colleague Mick Sharp and I waited, for example, at the Ring of Brodgar, Orkney, late one evening for precisely those circumstances, so did two other 'serious' photographers. We may or may not have been using the place for artistic purposes, but other uses include both commercial photography and overt art.

Ancient sites are often used photographically as suggestive locations for advertising. Standing stones in particular can be 'captured' to suggest mystery, strength, sexuality, venerability (Pl. 21). Stonehenge itself is the chief victim, but it recently faced competition from Avebury where an attempt was made to use the prehistoric stone circles, after hours and without permission, as a backdrop for a commercial advert featuring scantily-clad lovelies. Increasingly now such sites provide a location for video creations as well as still photography: we also shared the Ring of Brodgar with a crew making them. On what was clearly a busy, creative summer evening for the monument, someone else was painting, representative of the artistic stimulation ancient sites continue to provide just as they have for centuries. And, today, some artistic creativity is actually attempted on-site rather than just of the site. At Arbor Low, Derbyshire, for example, an outdoor fine art 'event' involving landscape art had left a shallow slot filled with orange jelly incised across the 4,000-year-old stone circle. Its traces could well puzzle archaeologists in future: a jelly-trench is not currently in the scholastic interpretative armoury.

Potentially even more confusing is the current artistic urge, associated with the name of Richard Long in particular, not so much to 'improve' existing monuments as to create new ones in the name of Art. Again stones tend to be the favoured material. They are used creatively to impose geometric patterns on the landscape: the line, the cross, the circle and the spiral. 'Placing five piles of stones along the way', for example, is the title of one of Long's works; 'Circle of crossing places' is another. 'Parallels for his work', we were informed by Nicholas Serota introducing Long's 1990 exhibition at the Tate, 'have been traced in the English landscape tradition of Constable and Nash, in the Taoist and Buddhist traditions of the Far East and in the signs and markings of the so-called "primitive" peoples, such as the Ancient Nazca Indians of South America or the Aboriginals of Australia.' In other words, post-modernism rules. 'However' ('however'? – author), 'his art is fundamentally rational in its concern with ... the place of man in the terrestial realm.' Much of his art is known, strictly speaking, only at second hand in the form of exhibition photographs of what he has created out of doors, but much of the Tate's central floor space was occupied in later 1990 by three originals, respectively 'Cornish Slate Line', 'Norfolk Flint Circle' and 'White Water Line'. Each took a day to make; anyone could easily spend a day looking and wondering what to make of them.

Pasts with people

In fact, during the hour I looked at them, I noticed most people just walked past, perhaps looking for Constable and Nash on the walls rather than recognising Art on the floor. But I was intrigued for, while my reaction to 'White Water Line' as a DIY disaster was presumably rooted in common experience, to me as an archaeologist the other two works conveyed images of 'monuments' deeply embedded in the British landscape. No need to look to the Far East, Australia or South America: 'Cornish Slate Line', a long, neatly-edged rectangle of split quarry-stone, spoke to me of the miles of laid track and tramway so arduously constructed across much of upland Britain in the eighteenth and nineteenth centuries to move in horse-drawn carts and tubs the minerals of thousands of mines and quarries to their point of departure for further processing and use. 'Norfolk Flint Circle', 10 m in diameter and so fresh in the patination of its large nodules, was surely inspired by (but was it?) sight of a freshly excavated Bronze Age funerary platform on East Anglian or Wessex chalk.

Andy Goldsworthy's *Slate Stack* (1986) at Little Langdale, Cumbria, a place resonating with archaeological significance for its associations with Neolithic stone-quarrying, consisted of a deeply satisfying pine-cone shape perched on its blunter end in a sea of slate debris. Such art need not of course be permanent: the same artist's 1990 *Hand to Earth* exhibition include 'Hole in Snow', 'a hole in a snow-covered Ingleborough hillside (on top of which is the highest hillfort in England) ... lined ... with peat to create an illusion of reversal and infinite depth' (G, 11 July). However, these creations are not necessarily the art itself, not least because they are of a particular place and somewhat limited portability. No, their purpose is often to be photographed; the image is removed and then, out on the cultural landscape, a new bit of what has presumably become detritus immediately after photography is left to clutter up the scenery – and mislead, though hopefully not for long, the field archaeologist. But, of course, the remains of this 'art' will themselves become 'monuments' in the sense of the title of this chapter with the passage of time. If any survive, as relics symptomatic of the late twentieth century, some will doubtless come to be preserved, not as art, but as archaeology.

Art plays on the emotions and it is they perhaps, rather than scientifically-controlled curiosity or just a sense of fun, that drive yet others to do things at monuments. A lot of people sense, even believe in, a pagan religiosity enwrapped in the ancient sites, again particularly stone circles. So they want to worship there, alone sometimes but usually as a group activity. The 'rites' of the Ancient Order of Druids at Stonehenge on the morning of midsummer's day is the best-known and most controversial example, but there are now other doubtless sincere but nevertheless rather vague religious happenings at other sites. Certainly evidence of contemporary events, in the form of fireplaces and Coke-cans for example, has appeared fairly widely at even the remotest of sites in recent years. Boleigh fougou in Cornwall, in the garden of the Centre for Alternative Education and Research, is used generally as a sort of pagan shrine and during the course 'Initiation – Rites of Passage'. Some similar uses may at least have a basis of folklore or tradition: at the stone circles on Stanton Moor, for example, fires lit on Halloween are associated with modern 'witches'.

Fires have also appeared *ad hoc* on ancient hilltop beacon sites, many of them almost by definition also possessing archaeological monuments. On at least two occasions of official national celebration in recent years – some Royal anniversary and the fourth centennial of the defeat of the Spanish Armada – fires and multitudes on the monuments occasioned temporary nocturnal fun and quite avoidable but permanent archaeological damage.

Some enquirers into the possible powers of ancient sites try to define their qualities more accurately by testing, for example, for geological, magnetic and electric anomalies. Maps are also used to claim geometric, even supernatural, symmetries in their incidence on the landscape. So, living pagan temples or bundles of lost knowledge alternate to received archaeological wisdom about them, the ancient monuments are alive again. In addition to all their 'proper' uses, they are also gathering places for their contemporary acolytes, challenging appreciation of their significance and the definition of their present-day function as limited by the 1979 Ancient Monuments Act.

Three other functions are similarly outside the Act. Again it is the accessibility and loneliness of the sites which lend them to abuse. Graffiti-making is a curious phenomenon in two respects. On the one hand, at the time it is done, and especially now, it is clearly a sort of vandalism in that it defaces a monument. Psychologically it is nevertheless presumably interesting, indicating motives ranging from extreme respect through a wish to share in something venerable to an out-and-out ego-trip probably with overtones of the anonymous individual seeking immortality.

Yet, on the other hand, whatever the motive, at some stage graffiti become part of the monument, meet to be likewise protected, preserved and even displayed. The official guide-books draw attention to the scratches made by a Norse visitor to the Ring of Brodgar. A present-day guided visitor to Maes Howe chambered tomb on Orkney, judging by my experience, is more likely to have his or her attention concentrated on the thousand-year-old graffiti of the Norse tomb robbers than the sophistication of the 5,000-year-old architecture of the tomb itself. At St Ninian's Cave in south-west Scotland, clearly a place of deep religious significance for many, the several thousand graffiti inscribed over centuries are vivid witness to the sanctity of what is in effect a Christian shrine. Additionally they provide a marvellous palimpsest of documentary evidence about the Cave's visitors and their lettering styles.

A contemporary analogue featured in the *Sunday Times Magazine* (19 August) under the headline 'Rave from the Grave'. 'Jim Morrison was the ultimate rock icon. Now his tomb is a graffitied shrine'; and the accompanying photograph of the grave in the Cimetière du Père-Lachaise, Paris, its aura of 'pimply squalor', its atmosphere 'as reverential as a belch', nevertheless shows a scene superficially of the same genre as that at St Ninian's Cave. The modern 'Visitors' Book' we are invited to sign as we enter historic house or ancient monument is of course a surrogate for such monumental scribbling.

The other two uses are less ambivalent in their anti-social nature. Contemporary archaeological evidence for drug-smoking on the ramparts of Dolebury, Avon, was mirrored at the other end of the country in a braggart entry about the activity in the visitors' book at Rennibister, Orkney, a suitably subterranean late-prehistoric chamber beneath a working farmstead. And who has not also inhaled that unmistakable smell of stale urine in castle dungeon or prehistoric burial chamber (Pl. 22)? The use of ancient monuments as public toilets is clearly one of their main purposes nowadays, in practice if not in intent. West Kennet long barrow, Wiltshire, appropriately roofed in lavatorial bottle-glass, is a favourite place of relief not far from the main A4 road; it also often contains evidence of its use for overnight camping. Perhaps, in the interests of hygiene, the realities of its concurrent functions should be faced and different burial chambers labelled accordingly. Judging by the number of times that this author and many others have also used the interior for television and radio programmes, another of these acoustically-excellent chambers might well be labelled 'recording studio'.

The managers and custodians of our deliberately-preserved heritage in the great outdoors have indeed a difficult task, coping with all this sort of activity incidental to their functions and to the primary purpose of the monuments as perceived now rather than then. What, one cannot help wondering, would the original builders and occupants have made of it all? But then, perhaps in many cases for all we know, the uses were as varied as they are now. It is precisely to enable thoughts like that to be aired, and possibly at some time answered, that, along with a host of other reasons, society puts so much contemporary effort into managing both the physical remains of its pasts and the meanings or images of those pasts.

1 New tourist heritage, official version 1990: the street furniture in Horse Guards Road, London, marking the entrance to the Cabinet War Rooms, exhibited by the Imperial War Museum.

2 The carefully tended ruins of Hadrian's Wall, the Roman Empire's north-west frontier, stretch east through a November landscape along the top of the Whin Sill cliff from Steel Rigg towards Housesteads fort in Northumberland. Crossing a World Heritage Site and National Trust property in a National Park, the public footpath is here part of the Pennine Way. A National Trail from North Sea to Irish Sea along the Wall is currently being devised by the Countryside Commission.

73

13　Maritime heritage, buses with their engines running and weary tourists in August: the *Cutty Sark* in the Royal Borough of Greenwich.

14　The rural idyll on a summer's morn in a Conservation Area: half-timbered, Georgian and Victorian houses, no traffic, distant cars parked outside shops and, nearer, their owners' dwellings and the village war memorial (1920) on the triangular-shaped Barber's Cross at the end of High Street, Watlington, Oxfordshire. Whatever the popular fantasies about this sort of image, this is a real photograph of a genuine scene, not of a pastiche, parody or theme park (May).

FRANKLIN

TO THE GREAT ARCTIC NAVIGATOR
AND HIS BRAVE COMPANIONS
WHO SACRIFICED THEIR LIVES IN COMPLETING
THE DISCOVERY OF THE NORTH WEST PASSAGE
A.D. 1847.8.
ERECTED BY THE UNANIMOUS VOTE OF PARLIAMENT

THIS HORSE BLOCK WAS ERECTED BY DESIRE OF
THE DUKE OF WELLINGTON 1830.

15   Society needs its heroes:
the Franklin monument,
Waterloo Place, St James's,
London.

16   The past selected for
preservation as heritage ranges
from the sublime to the
bizarre: in the national shrine
zone of St James's, London,
this ducally-desired horse-
mounting block on the edge of
a busy road outside The
Athenaeum was celebrating its
160th anniversary at the time
of the photograph (July),
despite a century of the
internal combustion engine.

17   A literary shrine: the Brontë Parsonage across the churchyard, Haworth, West Yorkshire, in March.

18   National heritage in typical form (July): the equestrian statue to King Edward VII, 'Rex Imperator', in Waterloo Place, London.

19 Escomb church, County Durham, is basically of Anglo-Saxon form and construction, its fabric incorporating stones from a nearby Roman fort. Of great architectural historical interest, it symbolises here the English parish church as a major component of the national heritage and a focal point in the pre-modern, local landscape (December).

20 Spontaneous but less scholarly construction by visitors 'improving' the past by piling up a modern cairn of stones robbed from the rampart of Carradale Point late prehistoric vitrified fort, Kintyre, Argyll.

21 The aesthetic, mysterious and possibly sexual appeal of the past as represented by the stark and lonely shapes of the Stones of Stenness, Orkney Mainland, the remains of a 4,000-year-old megalithic circle inside a henge monument, almost flattened but just visible as a surrounding ditch and outer bank.

22 The extraordinary length that official provision will make to preserve a monument *and* make it visitable is illustrated by Blackhammer Cairn, Rousay, Orkney, where the megalithic remains of a 5,000-year-old burial and ceremonial structure are secured beneath a modern concrete roof, incidentally making it a refuge for contemporary uses.

Past workings

Managing the past

7

The past does not just exist. What we see of its presence, and the uses that we make of our ideas about it, are to a considerable extent contrived.

The 'managing' of this chapter title is used in the contemporary sense of consciously intervening in the past and its effect on us, with the implicit understanding that such effort is made for 'the better'. That of course begs a lot of questions but making such value judgements is as unavoidable in the heritage field as in managing any other concern; and the decisions stemming from such judgements can of course have very different effects on a past or people today, even given that a decision was 'correct'. A decision to prevent public access to a preserved archaeological site or historic building, for example, on the basis of a value judgement that it was the last of its kind or very fragile, could disappoint, indeed even annoy, many people. A decision might be made, however, to open to the public and promote the availability of that same site or building, on the basis of a value judgement that the area it was in needed enhanced local interest for social reasons or more tourism for economic reasons. Such a decision could nevertheless equally both place the historic fabric at risk and upset a lot of other people. They would argue that such action would burn up the resource and that our generation's responsibility was one of stewardship rather than merely contemporary function. So, as with all good management, managing the past requires clear and well-judged policies based on much information and clearly defined priorities. The very large number of the interests involved, and the immense complexity of the field, however, ensure that virtually all heritage management occurs in a state of tension, not infrequently breaking out – or should it be 'down'? – into crisis management. The past is a very powerful liberator of misunderstanding, strong emotions – and large bills (e.g. Pls 1, 3, 6, 7, 8, 22, 28).

Management of the past is conducted at two levels. One concerns its physical presence, the other its intellectual form. Both are fundamentally affected by the institutions which do the managing.

Characteristically, the organisational structure dealing with the past is complex. It exists on global, international, continental, national, regional, district and local scales; one of its major pre-occupations is therefore not so much managing the past as attempting to co-ordinate the management of the past. Many of the plenitude of organisations, especially the large ones, are also inevitably much concerned with running themselves; the staff costs of English Heritage, for example, take up some 75 per cent of its budget. Management of the British heritage is inevitably bound up with supra-national organisations. For example, one of the great world bureaucracies, UNESCO, is the parent of the World Heritage Committee which receives nominations (41 in 1990) from the 115 states party to the World Heritage Convention. It selectively designates monuments and areas (372 so far) as 'World Heritage Sites'. Some, like Leptis Magna, are primarily archaeological. In Britain, currently with 13 such designations, the range is represented by the Giant's Causeway, St Kilda, the Stone-henge/Avebury areas, and Durham Cathedral and Castle, the last a rather special example of a tightly-knit, entirely architectural complex, grand but occupying only a small area. In contrast, the Hadrian's Wall World Heritage Site, stretching right across northern England, has no mapped limits. That such status is not easily obtained is exemplified by the English Lake District whose nomination has twice been deferred, in part because of fears about a possible decline in landscape quality through over-visiting. It is in good company: neither Ankor Wat, Jericho, Nimrud nor Babylon are designated either.

Britain's heritage management is also affected by the European dimension. Both the European Parliament and the Community are involved, fairly marginally to their main purposes but to considerable effect in the heritage field. The Council of Europe, for example, publishes an excellent free magazine, *A Future for Our Past*, intent on raising awareness of a European heritage. It also shows member states what they should or could be doing in their own territories, individually and as part of European initiatives. In north and west Europe the roots of heritage provision lie several centuries back, variously in post-Renaissance schol-arship, nascent patriotism and Royal patronage. In England, however, a medieval Royal interest was confined to the possible proceeds of treasure-hunting from ancient sites, a fact of which the influence is still perpetuated in the anachronistic and inadequate Treasure Trove procedure today. This covers only objects of gold and silver, and ownership of 'finds' often rests on a fine judgement of whether the objects were lost or deliberately hidden with intent to recover. In Scotland, however, 'the law requires that all newly discovered ancient objects, whether hidden or lost, belong to the Crown', a model which many believe should be extended to England and Wales (the quotation and that below are from *Hansard*, House of Lords, 13 December 1989, reproduced in *BAN* 6, 1, January 1991).

Despite many years of pressure, notably from the Council for British Archaeology, the government has once again refused to grasp the nettle of 'portable antiquities', quite deliberately now after engaging in public consultation on the matter three years ago. 'There is a valid public interest in some archaeological finds, but not all,' said its spokesman, Lord Hesketh; 'and there is a valid public interest in the knowledge represented by those finds, but not to the extent of requiring nationalization of finds in England and Wales.' So it proposes merely 'to seek ... a suitable legislative opportunity to amend the Ancient Monuments and Archaeological Areas Act 1979 to strengthen controls over finds from scheduled sites ...' and 'to promote improvements in the administration procedures not involving legislation and dealing with non-scheduled sites – one such option being a code of practice'. As the Director of the CBA commented, 'The heritage, in short, is up for grabs ... and whoever gets to it first can sell it to the highest bidder.' While it may seem regrettable to those concerned about the public and scientific interest in archaeological material that this should be the official position, its adoption represents a success for the treasure-hunting lobby in having achieved a political compromise in which, clearly, the integrity of the past has taken second place to contemporary reality. In that reality, such is the nature of much 'management' of the past.

This was exemplified again in the Department of the Environment's Planning Policy Guidance on *Archaeology and Planning* (PPG 16). Published in November, it was nevertheless undoubtedly one of the more important government statements in the field of archaeological resource management in recent years. Though without the force of law, it encapsulated much current practice but strengthened its role by clearly setting out what must now be regarded as officially-recognised 'good practice'. It stressed in particular the place of archaeological considerations in planning decisions and the need, therefore, by planning authorities for expert archaeological advice. Intended to 'strike the right balance between the needs of development and the interests of archaeology', the *Guidance* accepts the principle that archaeological remains are a finite, non-renewable resource, the basic concept of William Lipe's 'conservation model for archaeology' adumbrated in 1975 in the USA. It also makes clear that 'where nationally important archaeological remains and their settings are affected by proposed development, there should be a presumption in favour of their physical preservation' *in situ*.

Past workings

The point was explicitly referred to by Michael Heseltine as renewed Secretary of State for the Environment in refusing planning permission for a hotel complex at West Kennet Farm in the World Heritage Site of Avebury, Wiltshire (DoE News Release, 19 December). 'The Secretary of State concluded that the preference must be for the physical preservation of any remains where they lie as opposed to preservation by record.' He thereby not only supported the thrust of his own Department's *Guidance* but also relegated to the status of much inferior option the practice of 'preservation by record', a euphemism for destruction after all too often inadequate and incomplete archaeological excavation. With such an immediate and high-level application of the *Guidance* in so sensitive a context, hopes must be high for the improved management of the national archaeological resource in the 1990s. It will be most interesting to see how matters actually work out. Crucial players are the government itself, in managing its own estate and informing its many other actions which impinge on the historic environment, and planning authorities at local level.

Still at national level, this century the powers of the Crown were used (1906–10) to create three Royal Commissions on the Ancient and Historical Monuments of, respectively, Scotland, England and Wales, bodies charged with making inventories of the pre-1714 structures in their countries. The motive for this move was explicitly preservationist, it being correctly recognised that without knowledge of what existed it would be impossible to decide what was worthy of preservation. That principle holds good, though the attainment of the objective remains, as with hindsight we can see was bound to be the case, incomplete. Meanwhile the work of these bodies has expanded almost as exponentially as the philosophical and practical fields within which they operate.

Now the past has almost caught up with the present. Following the revision of the 1714 limit to 1945, recording work can extend to very recent buildings such as 'historic' cinemas and World War II installations, e.g. the contruction yards for Mulberry harbours. Furthermore, as those examples suggest, the range of that which is deemed to be 'representative of contemporary culture', to quote the Royal Commission's original Warrant, now stretches in time and type of site from the find-spot of a Palaeolithic flint axe through the fragmentary remains of a humble, medieval timber-framed building to Battersea power station. Yet few would query the appropriateness of recording as both 'historic' and 'significant', say, a Verulamium Roman theatre and Chatham dockyard, and what are the above examples but their recent counterparts? Nevertheless, disappointing and unsatisfactory though it is that the original, seemingly simple task of recording the ancient monuments and historic buildings of Britain is incomplete, the reality is that such a task is by definition uncompletable.

There is indeed a baffling ambivalence here: on the one hand, the argument for preservation must legitimately rest in part on the concept that our material survivals from the past are of a finite number, i.e. we cannot now add to the fixed number of items which happen to survive from the past. Yet, on the other hand, that is precisely what we do do, though only in a sense. While not actually increasing the number of sites, we appear to add to their number because we both make discoveries, i.e. of things which existed but which we did not know about, and we continuously give an historic significance to things which exist but which we had not counted because, up until whatever 'now' we are talking about, they had not been seen to be culturally significant.

The remains of the many thousands of late prehistoric and Romano-British settlements strewn across the English landscape, for example, all existed in 1900 though they were not known about; it required the intensification of post-World War II agriculture and the systematic application of archaeological air photography for their existence to be perceived. When the Commissions started, they naturally recorded large country houses and major urban buildings because, at the time, they were perceived to be important. Such is still the case but meanwhile, with the shift in contemporary society's perception of what is significant in its past, it has now become necessary to record the lesser, functional buildings around a country house and the streets of workers' housing (if they survive) peripheral to a municipal centre. The English Royal Commission is, for example, currently recording the 'historic' buildings in the areas of Urban Development Corporations, areas which by definition contain much that would not have been considered 'historic' even a few years ago. Yet various pasts represented by standing buildings in those areas are of considerable significance, nationally and locally, and the areas, also by definition, are seeing major changes in their fabric and functions.

Indeed, to take what may seem an extreme example is actually only to instance one with considerable implications for managing the past. When the Commissions started they were operating within the physical framework of the world's major industrial power. Now most of that power-base has gone and, with it, its physical presence. Much has been swept away, some replaced and built on. At best (in historical/archaeological terms) what survives does so fragmentarily, in redundant buildings, abandoned lines of transport and communications, and the fabric of derelict communities. Yet it is precisely the remains of this 'lost world' in which the Commissions began their work that now needs to be recorded. Not least is this so because they are of the world's major industrial power at the time, and that is clearly something which could not have been conceptualised in the unconscious dog-days of the Edwardian establishment. Nor does the process stop there: technological change in the twentieth century has tended to move faster and faster so that now, for example, first-generation nuclear power stations like Dounreay need to be recorded archaeologically as they in turn begin their long journey into redundancy. The past is very close behind us now.

In its recorded form, the past is publicly available in the National Monuments Record maintained by the three Royal Commissions. These are enormous archives of what has been recorded, a sort of national memory bank of Britain's heritage consisting of paper, photographic and computer files. They contain, for example, millions of air photographs and countless data about millions of historic buildings and archaeological sites. The chances are that some information about 'your' historic town or 'your' archaeological site will be there, recorded by parish and/or national grid reference. Certainly this will be the case with property which has an official existence as Listed Building and Scheduled Ancient Monument. The whole is in daily use by the official organisations concerned with the direct management of the heritage but the NMR, being public archives, have countless other uses too. Academics, picture researchers, authors, people just finding out what is held nationally about their own locality – these and many others are among the weekly visitors.

There are of course many other major national archives in the historic field. The national museums, for example, all have record functions too, with huge information archives supplementing their reserve collections of materials. The Map Room at the British Museum is just one example of an incomparable resource within a huge complex. Sooner or later, most researchers end up at the Public Record Office. And other institutions outside official provision contribute significantly to what the nation holds about its history. The library of the Royal Institute of British Architects is one outstanding example, with irreplaceable original architects' drawings. Complementing this national provision is of course a local record resource. Most counties in England have a Record Office and, now, all also have a Sites and Monuments Record, characteristically maintained in the County Council Planning Department under the direction of a county archaeologist. Much the same is true of Scotland at regional level, though in Wales the function is largely discharged through the independent regionally-based Archaeological Units.

The development of this coverage across Britain, and its direct involvement with the work of the planning authorities over the last twenty years, has been and is one of the significant success stories in the management of the archaeological resource. It depends on the continuous enhancement of the quality of the Sites and Monuments Records and, though they can always be improved, information about what exists where, and its significance, is better organised and consequently more readily available than at any time in the past. This happy conjunction of principle, professionalism and practical need has arisen through a partly planned, partly serendipitous, co-operation of central and local government, with English Heritage playing a pioneering role in the 1980s. Now, in England, the Royal Commission has been recognised by government as having the lead role in the sense of being generally responsible for standards, compatibility and integration of what in essence, however and wherever it may be held, are the components of the national heritage record.

Most of the rest of the official state organisational structure in Britain is a parliamentary creation, essentially stemming from a series of Ancient Monuments and Town and Country Planning Acts. The Ancient Monuments and Archaeological Areas Act, 1979, is currently in force, though the latter provision, a botched attempt to incorporate the Town and Country Planning concept of Conservation Areas into Ancient Monuments legislation, has not been extended beyond half a dozen historic cities and is officially under review. Political responsibility in England rests with the Secretary of State for the Environment, and general provision with his Department. The executive agency is the quasi-autonomous Historic Buildings and Monuments Commission for England, not to be confused with the similarly-named Royal Commissions and so seeking a popular personality by calling itself 'English Heritage' (initially rather to the annoyance of other heritage organisations, especially those whose remit embraced a wider meaning, or was in different fields, of heritage).

In Wales and Scotland, similar functions are carried out by divisions still part of the Civil Service, namely of the Welsh Office and the Scottish Development Department, while in Northern Ireland the statutory functions and the recording work both lie within the Department of the Environment. This lack of consistency is entirely characteristic of the way things are organised 'nationally' in the UK, reflecting the three strands of different historical developments, the politics of nationalism, and the general theory of administration by cock-up. While in part that can be explained away as historical accident in the case of 'monuments and historic buildings', a similar organisational inconsistency between the different countries of the UK, this time in the countryside and nature conservation field, has been deliberately perpetrated by the British government during 1990 and is being put into operation in 1991. Welcome 'English Nature': may 'Welsh' birds and 'Scotch' mists respect your national boundaries, nor the Irish Sea erode them.

The executive functions of English Heritage are fairly wide, backed up by an annual budget of some £80 million. The brief is to look after, and encourage public participation in, the built heritage. In practice this involves a considerable advisory role, not least to owners of monuments and historic buildings. The making of many finely-judged assessments is basic to a grant-giving role; public access, often on about thirty days per year, is a condition of grant, for example towards the maintenance of an historic house or the structures in an historic garden. Such grants are typically of the order of 25 per cent of the cost. English Heritage also directly maintains some 350–400 monuments in its own care; most are open to the public for most of the year. These are usually discrete sites with only small areas of land around them; Stonehenge on its little triangle of land is typical of many, often castles and religious ruins but also including some Roman and prehistoric sites. Several prehistoric sites and a museum scattered in and around Avebury, St Peter's Church, Barton-upon-Humber, Chysauster 'Ancient Village', Dover Castle, Maiden Castle hillfort, Portchester Castle, a medieval merchant's house at Southampton, the multi-period settlement at Wharram Percy, North Yorkshire, Tintagel of bogus Arthurian fame on the Cornish cliffs, and Wroxeter Roman town give a flavour of the range of sites involved.

Some are 'open' at all times, that is they are unstaffed; at most, however, the visitor will be greeted nowadays by a customer-friendly custodian, cheerful in Hardy-Amies-designed country-style uniform, trained to charge for entry with a smile and equipped with financial incentive and soft-sell vocabulary to recruit another member apparently to the organisation but actually to a parallel sort of supporters' club.

'Remember, wherever you live or go on holiday in England, you are never far from an English Heritage property' is part of the invocation to membership, linking with English Heritage's third area of executive action, in its own words 'to *use* this glorious inheritance'. Perhaps to do so is seen as part of managing the past and certainly managing this function is an important part of the organisation's activities.

Among other official, national bodies, together handling millions of pounds of public money are the National Museums and the National Heritage Memorial Fund. Of the former, the British Museum is without equal, an institution really to be proud of yet, like the other national museums, also currently plagued by problems which are more to do with political culture-mongering than the niceties of scholarship and permanent curatorship. 'Management' is, somewhat ironically, a word frequently used in these controversies. It means in this context that the government wants it and the others run, not necessarily 'well' in the sense of 'appropriate to their particular purposes' but in a particular way with the emphases on 'cost-effectiveness' and 'value for money', now with the 'money' of course coming increasingly from private rather than public sources. As the job description for the Directorship said (January 1991), 'The Trustees look to continue the Museum's successful record of raising sponsorship for special displays and towards the refurbishment of public galleries.' Hence the public arguments about charging for entry – and the current British Museum Director's brave and public threat to resign rather than agree – and the interest in the Science Museum's drop to two-thirds in its visitor numbers since charging was introduced there.

Hence too the heated public exchanges over management reorganisation, in effect a down-grading of the status and influence of curators in relation to administrators, in the national museums, the Victoria and Albert Museum and the Science Museum in particular. In October 1990, the Director of the latter eloquently voiced an alternative interpretation of the situation at a prestigious international conference in London on 'Museums and Scholarship' under the auspices of the Royal Society for Arts, sponsored by Fiat. That the conference was held at all was vivid demonstration of the presence of concern about the past in contemporary society, though the cynic may well have seen it as a put-up job by the London cultural mafia outraged by what it sees as the betrayal of (its) scholarly values in current changes at the national museums in London. Berlin, Paris and New York, similar museological centres of excellence, were paraded as exemplars sticking to traditional museum ideologies based first and last on scholarship.

Neil Cossons, Director of the Science Museum, pointed out, however, that given the very much changed socio-economic circumstances in which the British national museums now operate, the challenge was to control change as the only sensible alternative to being swamped by it. Ultimately, he argued, the bringing in of professional managers, fund-raisers, marketing specialists and public relations experts, as part of a team with the curators would, by enabling the museums to survive and develop, preserve and enhance that scholarship on which they were based. The scholarly curators, however, had to accept the principle of teamwork in a new situation in which their traditional organisational supremacy had been overtaken by the need for a range of specialists to manage a national museum.

The logic is persuasive, no more indeed than an extension of what has been happening for decades in museum work. First specialist subject curators replaced the all-knowing single curator, then figures such as scientific conservators, designers and education officers supplemented the academic staff in response to opportunities and public demands. Though of little comfort to curators who have been sacked in the shake-up, a similar process is happening in other institutions, not least in universities where, while 'hard-core' academics are persuaded to take early retirement and their posts are 'frozen', Registrars' departments blossom with new appointments in the 'soft' activities of PR, fund-raising and information dissemination.

In the heritage field generally, not just in national museums, behind the political and financial imperatives bringing this situation to a head lie more fundamental issues of management. At stake is the very nature of 'the managed past' itself. In part, of course, the question is simply 'What sort of past can we afford?'; though in practice, since we could spend as much money on the past as we wanted to if we were prepared to accept the consequences, the question is rather 'What sort of past can we fashion with x per cent of the GNP?' Given limited resources, clearly they have to be managed; it is easy enough to add 'to good effect' or 'to give value for money' but that begs the questions of who takes the decisions and why the decision-makers take the decisions that they do. On those decisions depends that nature of the past that is preserved, projected and made available. Who is it meant for? Why some rather than others? And by what right do a few decide what the 'heritage' of a nation, a region, a locality, should be?

Superficially, the management of museums, national or otherwise, has little to do with countryside management yet both are linked in some common questions about heritage management. The English love-affair with the countryside has already been mentioned (above p. 39); yet there, as with museums in some respects, the management of that as heritage has produced a consumable alien to a significant minority of British citizens. This point of view was most helpfully voiced by an environmental education co-ordinator in a London education authority (*Countryside Commission News*, September/October). 'I am a "normal" person', he says, yet on Loughrigg Fell in the Lake District with a group of school children, he provoked reactions from fell walkers and others ranging 'from staring to subdued, or not so subdued, chatter'. Why? – after all, 'I was carrying a map [and] wearing the correct clothing and boots.' Julian Agyeman is black, and he wrote of 'a feeling of alienation' in visiting the countryside, 'a perception that it is "not for us" ...' He quoted a friend for whom 'a visit to the countryside is always accompanied by a feeling of unease. ....' Similar reactions must be experienced by most members of ethnic minorities in Britain visiting museums: they are not for them, unconsciously so maybe, but nevertheless. There is a profound issue here for all managers of heritage, whatever form it may take.

Not necessarily with racial overtones but similarly, survey after survey shows that the traditional museum, product of largely unconscious management of what the past should consist of, is a no-go area for numerically large sectors of the public they are ostensibly supposed to be for. White, middle-class literate values, making assumptions about what people want and should know about the past and relying heavily on a visual, intellectual relationship between the viewer and the shown, underlie many a display. But what if the visitor is visually underdeveloped, i.e. does not know what to look for or cannot read the signals given out from a particular exhibition format? A sherd of common-or-garden Roman pottery, actually held in the hand, may well meet his or her needs, may well provide a 'significance', better than the most elaborately displayed, but encoded, precious artefact 'explained' by subtle side-lighting and 500 words of scholarly prose. Some museums are addressing issues of this kind, for example the Archaeological Resource Centre of the York Archaeological Trust, but clearly management of the past includes far more than its organisational structure. The components of it should all the time be cross-examined with questions, not just about what they are *not* doing, but about *why* they do what they *are* doing.

National heritage is then a particularly sensitive concept; to invent a new body ostentatiously called the National Heritage Memorial Fund would seem to be offering a hostage to fortune. The NHMF in Britain is a recent and idiosyncratic organisation, but one with a key role in national heritage provision. Essentially, it consists of up to eleven Trustees with only a few full-time staff; it holds at least the memory of the Land Fund, set up to commemorate the dead of two World Wars in the late 1940s but never actually implemented in terms of its money being used for national commemorative purposes. Converted into its present form and given an initial capital fund under the National Heritage Act 1980, its job is to identify those parts of the national heritage worthy of grant aid and to administer grants to them, mainly through other bodies. Dodging the philosophical issues, its Chairman in effect defined what it should be spending its money on, that is the national heritage, as that on which it spends its money. As the former Secretary to the Trust wrote, 'The national heritage is now a seamless robe.'

The results of this splendidly pragmatic approach were to be seen in a special exhibition at the British Museum in 1988. In the forecourt was a World War I Mark IV tank, *Flirt II* (military), while inside exhibits ranged from Fine Art such as Tintoretto's *Deposition of Christ*, through fine art such as Bewick's original blocks for his woodcuts, to chunks of historic machinery and photographs of country houses and landscape. The exhibition *Catalogue* neatly defined not so much what had come to be 'national heritage' as what 'national heritage' had come to mean: great houses, landscaped parks and gardens, churches and ecclesiastical monuments and fittings, great art, 'portraits of nature', memorabilia of great persons such as writers, musicians and explorers, historic industrial places and equipment, militaria, archaeological objects preferably of gold, silver or artistic worth, and 'movies, piers and postcards'. All had been acquired with the help of NHMF grants but were held or owned locally. While all society benefits from such eclecticism, one of the main beneficiaries, on behalf of that society as it were, was and is the other major national heritage body, the National Trust.

There are in fact two National Trusts in the UK, one for Scotland which is quite small though significant in that country, and *The* National Trust embracing England, Wales and Northern Ireland. The latter enrolled, almost incredibly, its two millionth member in August 1990. The size of this membership gives it the distinction of being the largest conservation organisation in the world. A logistical consequence is that it now costs some £100,000 and takes several weeks for the Trust to communicate by post with its own members. Another handicap is that, because of its name, size and conspicuous wealth, it is all too often perceived to be 'official' and well-off; yet it is in fact an entirely voluntary and independent organisation with no entitlement to government or any other public funds. Its moneys come from members' subscriptions (the crucial bedrock one-third of its annual income), investment, rents, benefactions, endowments, donations, grants and any profits from its trading operation, National Trust Enterprises Ltd (teas and perfume-filled shops a speciality).

As it enters the 1990s, the Trust, the largest private landowner in Britain, needs about £80 million a year just to keep going at its current level of estate management, conservation, trading and membership servicing. Even so, highly professional organisation that it is with a staff now of well over two thousand, it depends very much in its field operations upon volunteers, notably in opening hundreds of properties to the public every year. Some twenty thousand volunteers now give the Trust about a million hours of their time each year.

In fact, from the global to the local level, much of the activity in looking after our various pasts depends on volunteers. Indeed, they initiate much of the action, looking to their own pasts rather than merely subscribing with their efforts to other pasts defined by official agencies and national organisations. It may well be, in yet another of those curious heritage paradoxes, that increasingly the big battalions will be tending to manage their pasts for the intellectually and physically passive, the consumers, while commitment will synchronously tend to express itself as participation in local and personal activity. If so, management of the past has yet to address its most serious challenge. Meanwhile, as the ubiquity, significance and nature of heritage come increasingly to be taken aboard as factors in management within an organisationally complex network, the management of heritage management itself is becoming a challenge in its own right.

8 | *Past practicalities*

'Had a good day at the monument, dear?' is not the homecoming question asked merely of those few hundred archaeologists, architects and custodians who have legitimately spent their working hours of a day at an ancient or historic site. Nowadays it could as well be asked of one of the not-so-small army of heritage managers and administrators, people not necessarily with any academic background or even any particular commitment to archaeology, history or learning. 'Running the past' in the present can be just another job and, in practice, many of its elements are similar to those of other fields of activity.

Estimates and budgets, cash-flows, corporate plans and mission statements are as much a part of heritage management as they are of managing any other business. Especially is this so when large organisations are involved or when those concerned are themselves only a small part of such an organisation, perhaps in existence primarily for other purposes, for example a local authority. Nevertheless, tricky practical problems are a feature of managing the heritage and, almost without exception, behind them lie both wider and deeper issues of a societal, philosophical and ethical nature. Archaeology has often been compared to both detective and surgical work; in its public and professional role, the parallels in such matters are much closer than those who make the flip methodological analogies realise. They will sometimes emerge as we look at some practicalities.

'Ancient Monuments' are not just any old site but, strictly speaking and with capital letters, one sort of official monument. To become one, a site has to be more than old: it has also to have been recognised as of 'national importance' and to have been entered on a Schedule, that is a list maintained by English Heritage on behalf of the Department of the Environment (and by the Historic Building and Monuments Directorate, Scottish Development Department, and CADW, Welsh Office). 'Scheduled', according to the Scottish HBMD information leaflet, 'means simply that a monument is sufficiently important to be included in a set of records maintained by the Secretary of State' but of course the whole point of the creation of such a set of records is to define 'Scheduled Ancient Monuments' as those archaeological sites with an official, bureaucratic existence geared to its protection (Pl. 23).

The same leaflet gives a classic, fourfold negative as to what scheduling does *not* do. It does not imply that the monument is threatened or poorly maintained; that the owner/occupier has any obligation for upkeep; that the Secretary of State is assuming responsibility; or that any right of access is being created. Negativism lurks still as it changes to the positive in stating that 'the main effect of scheduling is to try to ensure that nothing done on a scheduled monument will inadvertently alter its characteristics, damage or destroy it'. Proceeding to the key management provision, it then explains that owners and occupiers must obtain the Secretary of State's consent, 'normally ... in advance', if they wish to carry out work on a Scheduled Ancient Monument. The legal requirement for 'Scheduled Monument Consent', inevitably SMC on a SAM, was the main improvement contained in the 1979 Act, bringing SAMs into line with the provision for Listed Buildings under the Town and Country Planning Act (Pl. 24).

About fourteen thousand SAMs are designated in England. Official policy in the 1990s is to increase their number to some sixty thousand, an estimated 10 per cent sample of the total number of archaeological sites known to exist in England alone. Whatever the validity of the size and nature of that sample, this is an enormous task for, apart from getting the archaeology right, the product must be documented in such a way that any one item on the Schedule can, in the last resort, stand up to cross-examination in a court of law. Clearly the whole project raises issues of logistics, resources, professional skills, property rights (there is no appeal against a proposal to Schedule), site-management and different concepts of 'national heritage'. Further, the whole needs to be based on sharply-defined and consistent criteria within a theoretical framework which nevertheless allows for change as both experience and new knowledge affect ideas not just about which sites should be Scheduled Monuments but what a Scheduled Monument ought to be.

Scheduling as such does not provide right of public access so most visitors to archaeological sites will be going to one of the four hundred or so 'Properties in Care' (formerly Guardianship Monuments) looked after by English Heritage on behalf of the public. Comparable destinations could be among the fifty or more archaeological monuments open to the public by the National Trust (which would almost certainly be Scheduled too). A small number of archaeological monuments belonging to other bodies, such as National Parks, local authorities and private organisations, are also open to the public. The prime objective of all, except possibly the last, is to maintain the site academically and structurally as an historic or 'ancient' monument while allowing, indeed positively encouraging, people to visit it.

Many a maintained property has come, however, to have other functions, some official, many not so. Simply to exist, preserving historic integrity and scientific interest, providing moments of quiet contemplation for those genuinely interested in the past, is deemed insufficient justification for their being; they have to earn their keep. Furthermore, their very historicity has attracted other uses in an increasingly leisured, and perhaps even bored, society. In this context, too, it may well be their isolation, their open space and their public access, rather than their oldness or historic interest, which provide the magnet and the opportunity.

Some uses are themselves age-old. Ancient sites have in many cases existed, as they still do, in farmed landscapes (Pl. 25), so they tend to be used normally in the course of farming without real intent to damage. Many sites, including supposedly protected ones, have been ploughed over. Thousands have been flattened in this way, ironically producing a major harvest of archaeological discoveries through systematic aerial photography since the 1960s: we have learnt as we have destroyed, not least in 1990 when the dry summer produced archaeological crop-marks in quantity and of considerable significance (not to be confused with the controversial 'crop-circles' simultaneously appearing in the same cereal medium). The shape of many preserved sites, recognised as existing because they protrude up into the landscape as earthworks or stone structures, has nevertheless been altered by the modern practice of plough-ing right up to and even on to ancient mounds and banks during farming's phase of grabbing every square metre of land that could be made productive. The less intensive demands of pastoral farming, on the other hand, have by and large been compatible with the survival of archae-ological sites; indeed, sheep-grazing is one of the best forms of land-management from an archaeological point of view, though the same is not true of use by cattle and pigs (Pl. 26). In general terms, an archaeology in Britain which, until the eighteenth century, is very much about farming has since had to survive with agricultural land-use as best it can. Its deliberate preservation is a relatively recent development, in part because of the intensification of agricultural land-use itself.

In the countryside many good habitation sites are reused, thankfully for the study of the past since continued use, or reoccupations, add very considerably to the archaeological interest. Avebury itself is a good example, with the medieval village spreading into the Neolithic enclosure;

more remotely, but typically, the hut circles of prehistoric farmers at Llyn Llagi in north Wales were reused as foundations for medieval farm buildings. Neolithic chambered cairns, too, have been used as cattle stalls and stables. Capel Garmon is one such; East Bennan cairn on Arran is used as an area for spreading out hay to feed cattle – a perfectly natural thing to do, for the cairn material makes the area higher and drier than the surrounds. Cattle appreciate the advantages of a mound too, especially on hot days when they can enjoy a bit of updraught, and who are they to distinguish between mounds natural and man-made? Similarly with standing stones: can we expect a cow to differentiate between, on the one hand, a rubbing stone specifically placed in the centre of a newly-enclosed field in the nineteenth century AD for the scratchy delectation of its predecessors and, on the other, a ceremonial pillar erected in the nineteenth century BC? Sheep also love wearing windbreaks out of grassy slopes and, even more so with their brain-power, is it reasonable to expect them to tell the difference between natural scarp and hillfort rampart?

And does such a difference matter anyway, to humans such as the average dog-walker rather than animals? A hilltop is often an open space with fine paths for striding along whether or not it is enclosed by a hillfort: such hilltops merely provide especially good paths atop the ramparts. Nevertheless, while important uses of monuments in farming and in providing contemporary amenity can be acknowledged, the wear and tear of the latter apparently more innocent use can seriously damage the structure of a monument. Wear and tear may be less dramatic than destruction by plough but its insidiousness is in fact its danger. A worn path may, for example, initiate erosion. Though this is now a well-known phenomenon, wearing away some of the world's great, and most visited, monuments such as the Acropolis, the process applies to a lesser or greater extent wherever people regularly visit sites. At Barbury Castle, Wiltshire, and Uffington Castle, Oxfordshire, for example, both hillforts on chalk in areas of shallow topsoil and fragile turf, considerable management effort has had to be devoted to visitor control in as unobtrusive ways as possible lest the sheer leisure use of the sites damages their appearance and structure irretrievably.

Dog-walking, picnicking, kite-flying and the like are, however, essentially benign. Even playing games need not be archaeologically damaging, though people might object on other grounds. The posts on Crickley Hill, Gloucestershire (Pl. 27), for example, mark excavated Iron Age features, not goalposts, yet the settlement areas between the late prehistoric and Neolithic ramparts is regularly used for informal football (in a Country Park, never mind an Ancient Monument). Still, organised cricket is played within the Roman walls of Portchester on a millennium of archaeological stratification and golf intermeshes with prehistoric and Roman earthworks on numerous courses, for example on Bathampton Down, Bath, and Haltwhistle Common, Northumberland (not always to the benefit of archaeology, it might be added). Less formally, despite the notices not to climb on walls, many an ancient site with standing structures, like Clickhimin, Shetland, in effect serves as a sort of adventure playground for children. Presumably it is the risk of falling, or being hit by a loosened stone, which prompts English Heritage to include on its official site notice boards the somewhat gnomic statement that 'Ancient Monuments can be dangerous'.

Walking itself becomes a different matter when thousands of people do it along the same line. The problems of the Pennine Way and other long-distance routes are well known; they become magnified archaeologically when such numbers understandably want to walk along a linear monument such as Offa's Dyke between England and Wales and Hadrian's Wall. In recent years, hundreds of thousands of pounds have been spent on maintenance and restoration along the latter because of people's natural tendency to walk along its actual top; now the Countryside Commission is planning an official walk along the Wall which is hardly likely to diminish the problem (Pl. 12). Typical of the sort of even larger problem that the mega-sites seem to attract, especially if they are in a National Park or of World Heritage status – and the Hadrian's Wall frontier is both – are applications for planning approval to test-drill for oil in their vicinity.

The practicality of managing the past involves countless minor examples of threats and erosion. Long-distance paths are identifiable, but the wear and tear of local paths can easily and suddenly threaten to damage an archaeological site too. People love to walk over the top of burial mounds, for example, and thousands of feet can steadily wear a gully into the mound material; a heavy rainstorm and, before you know where you are, erosion has taken place. Mam Tor, in the Peak National Park, is a classic case: both archaeological excavation of, and a massive new flight of steps over, the ramparts had to be completed here to offset the effects of thousands and thousands of people understandably wanting to reach the top – for the view, let it be said, not the archaeology. Nor need the threat be people: marine erosion is one of the biggest and most expensive factors affecting many sites, especially round the Scottish coasts and islands (Pl. 28). Inland, horse-trails can be a quite different factor in creating the conditions for erosion to start. Hillforts again naturally provide excellent conditions for riding, exemplified by Uleybury, Gloucestershire, but Thelwell has much to answer for archaeologically. Even the 'normal' ground disturbance of a hunt meeting, as horses, hounds and people milled around, did not exactly further the well-being of the Altarnun Nine Stones, a prehistoric stone circle in Cornwall.

The combined effects of uncontrolled over-use of a public amenity with an archaeological basis by walkers, horses, cars, four-wheel-drive vehicles, tractors and motorbikes is all-too-sadly illustrated along the Ridgeway between Avebury and Barbury in Wiltshire, supposedly but incorrectly labelled as 'the oldest road in the country/world' (see p. 36). Yet where do you draw the line? On nearby Oldbury hillfort people were simultaneously scrambling their motorbikes over and between the ramparts, flying radio-controlled model aeroplanes, and mushroom-picking – all enjoying themselves and respectively disturbing the archaeology, the aural environment and the flora.

Using wheeled vehicles can of course disturb all three. The traditional enemy here has been the military to whom visible archaeological monuments have proved irresistible, quite apart from the damage done to many invisible ones. Hillfort ramparts and prehistoric burial mounds on Salisbury Plain were preferred sufferers, as gun-fire targets, tank obstacles and slit-trench locations. That situation is now officially under control but the leisure threat of four-wheel-drive vehicles has broken out elsewhere. On Rough Tor, Bodmin Moor, for example, four-wheel-drive 'bean tins' were driven through the (Scheduled) prehistoric settlement, converted for the day into a sort of yuppies' (or were they yobbos?) playground; while the same Tor is used as a check point for Naval cadets on a training march. Surrogate militarism was represented at the late prehistoric cemetery of Danes Graves, Humberside, by the discarded, empty cartridges of war-games played in the wood covering the burials. And whatever may have been achieved at Stonehenge over the last decade, presumably the midsummer occasions have provided useful exercises in dealing with civilians for the military, the police and private security organisations.

Some of these 'heritage police' had to be called once more to Stonehenge on 23 September, when early morning visitors sought to celebrate the autumnal equinox; and again when they were able to enjoy an expensive (for English Heritage) day-out at the monument at the midwinter solstice in December, but not many people joined them.

One of the practical curiosities about Stonehenge is that, while the monument itself and its little triangle of land between the main roads is managed by English Heritage, all the other land round about is owned by the National Trust. The Trust is imbued with the ethos of management, notably in the sense of estate management. As it has taken aboard an awareness of its archaeology, most of which was acquired unknowingly, the thousands of sites and landscapes involved have therefore been absorbed into a well-founded and increasingly sophisticated system of land management within the concept of the 'estate' as a whole. A similar development has occurred within other particular constituents of that 'estate', i.e. the whole of the Trust's properties, such as nature conservation, gardens, libraries and tapestries. The Duchy of Cornwall is another great but fragmented estate to have put a similar, holistic policy into place.

This form of integrated estate management stems from a centuries-old tradition of the great land-owners, now regularised by professional training and standards. Its ability to perform well depends crucially upon an ever-increasing data-base of what exists on the estate and how it is best managed. This is whence the dynamic tension driving so much of the Trust's activities derives. On the one hand, its estate is a living one on which rural livelihoods, landscape appearance and very necessary rental income depend while, on the other, the Trust's purpose is conservation in the public interest. Its objectives, constitution and privileges are, after all, defined in an Act of Parliament. Inevitably, therefore, clashes of interest occur, not rarely or as a weakness in the Trust, but all the time and as a strength; for, as a matter of daily fact, the Trust's approach involves the identification and resolution of such conflicts within a clearly-defined management framework.

The sort of clash in mind is easily exemplified. A 200-year-old hardwood plantation in a country house park needs, in silvicultural terms, surgical attention and partial replanting. It is, however, a key visual element in the late eighteenth-century historic parkland so beloved of the visiting aesthete, though documentary research shows a differently shaped plantation to have existed fifty yards east of it in Repton's original design. Which should be 'restored'? Furthermore, the lichens on some of the old bark are being used as the test-beds in a long-term study of aerial pollution funded by the National Environmental Research Council, and the Trust's own Biological Survey has identified the plantation's present semi-derelict condition as the northernmost known habitat of Dickie's Bladder Fern (or whatever). The rookery is considered to add much to the ambience of the place, and there remains the question of whether the small folly in the undergrowth was built as a ruin by the Ninth Earl or, like him, merely became one.

Likewise, a tenant on an upland sheep farm quite reasonably proposes to flatten the redundant earth and stone dykes on his rough grazing, replace them with stock-proof barbed-wire fencing to form efficient new fields for cattle, and put down a new ley to increase his stocking capability, thus making his highly marginal farm economically more viable (with a higher rent to the Trust of course). The dykes, however, happen to be a particularly good example of late-medieval assarting, incorporating structural elements from a rare type of prehistoric land allotment recently recorded by the Trust's Archaeological Survey. Associated with it are the hitherto unrecognised but remarkably well-preserved remains of a Romano-British settlement on which two of the new fences would meet. Clearly, this 'ancient landscape' provides the context for the well-known Tiddler's Tump, a single Bronze Age burial mound Scheduled under the Ancient Monuments Act and therefore 'of national importance'; though it is probably more significant locally as the place where, in the eighteenth century, the vicar, the Rev. Augustus Tiddler, met the squire's daughter on the night of their elopement. The public right of way to the Tump, claimed by some also to be a leyline, would have to be diverted around the new fields. In addition, the rubble core of the dykes provides a favoured residence of small mammals on which the tenuously re-established two breeding pairs of sparrow-hawks depend for their food supply.

Such complexities, individually from real life though here compounded into fictional examples, test both the management system and collective judgement all the time. The 'estate management' approach does not always work; mistakes occur, for both humans and systems are fallible. Furthermore, a 'correct' decision today can prove only too easily to be misjudged twenty-five years later, a factor of no little importance in the context of the long-term perspective of the Trust's heritage management. It is, after all, concerned with the forever in as far as that is conceptually possible; yet all the time is having to make decisions now, any one of which and certainly all together fashion the nature and image of our heritage as we perceive it and as posterity will receive it.

The very dynamics of this consciously holistic approach contrast markedly with much that was, and in some cases still is, basic in former attempts at heritage management. The whole idea of an Ancient Monument, for example, led to a particular method of 'preserving' each one individually as a separate 'thing', isolated from its environmental, topographical, cultural and sociological context (Pl. 29). Nowhere is this better illustrated than at that focus of contemporary activity, that mirror of contemporary society, Stonehenge.

The stone circle was given by its then owner to the state early in the twentieth century; its ownership is now vested in the Secretary of State for the Environment and it is managed on his behalf by English Heritage. Apart from the small triangle of land between three roads on which it sits, all the surrounding land was acquired by public subscription in the 1920s and belongs to the National Trust which has properly declared it 'inalienable', i.e. it can only be taken for purposes other than the Trust's by a decision of parliament. The Trust characteristically regards its land as its Stonehenge estate and manages it as such, recently bringing about major changes in land-use, access, visual improvement and archaeological protection. The great monument now enjoys a landscape setting appropriate to it, certainly better than was the case even ten years ago and very definitely an improvement on the situation in the 1920s (Pl. 1).

Immediately beside it, however, are facilities for the three-quarters of a million visitors each year which are entirely inappropriate (Pl. 30). The stone circle itself, which those visitors cannot normally now enter (cf. Pl. 32) is surrounded by a combination of tarmac path and a zone of heavy erosion. These delights are reached from an unpleasant carpark, via a tatty reception area with snack bar, through a brutalist, urban-style underground tunnel decorated with information boards somewhat unconducive to the creation of feelings of respect, never mind awe, at the prospect of standing where ancestors felt both four thousand years ago.

Plans for a better-managed Stonehenge have been under discussion for decades; currently they envisage a prestigious Visitor Centre a kilometre to the north, thus forcing visitors to approach on foot from the direction in which the designers of the megalithic temple intended their great structure to be viewed to greatest effect. Such plans, however, depend crucially on roads: the closing of the A344 which currently severs the monument from its Avenue, and the building of a new road to the proposed new Centre. Local people object to the former; the latter would have to cross inalienable land, would unavoidably intrude into a World Heritage Site, and inevitably promises to contribute significantly in pushing the development costs of the whole project beyond what is reasonable even for a unique monument of world class. The currently-quoted figure of some £15 million might in any case put the project beyond what is practicable, even given massive donations and sponsorship.

Meanwhile, a new player on the Stonehenge scene is creeping up from the wings. The upgrading to dual carriageway of the existing A303 trunk road immediately to the south of the monument will occur in the 1990s. Quite apart from the major implications of the works in terms of archaeological destruction and necessary surveillance, however they are carried out and to whatever design, the impact of this development on a sacred and much-visited landscape will be severe aurally and visually unless a considerable investment of skill and public money is made to mitigate it, for instance by sinking and covering the new dual carriageway in a tunnel. At one level, the question can be asked as to whether the Ministry of Transport will be willing to make that investment; but at another, the management issue here is essentially, as with so much else about Stonehenge, a political one.

Consideration of Stonehenge is unavoidable for its own sake; but the site and its landscape also so often seem so accurately to exemplify general problems and illustrate wider issues. In management terms, it demonstrates vividly that the past physically existing in the present requires far more of a reaction than merely 'saving' a monument and then opening it to the public. In acute form, it illustrates the practicalities of split management, visitor pressure, competing claims, the wider setting, various designations, legal ownership and statutory provision, and access at various levels of meaning. More subtly, it begs questions of appropriateness, style, academic knowledge, presentation and interpretation, aesthetics and ethics. In so doing, it makes the point that management, and especially mismanagement, are involved with all such matters, making demands far beyond those of mere organisation and day-to-day operating efficiency. Political and philosophical questions lie not far below the surface of Stonehenge today: 'What is it for in the late twentieth century?' quickly becomes 'Who is it for in the twenty-first century?' as soon as you start considering whether to put a visitor centre of any particular sort in one place rather than another.

The presence of such philosophical issues, and their attempted resolution or avoidance by the making of value judgements, are not of course particular to the management of archaeological heritage. They lurk in the management of wider fields of heritage too. The Countryside Commission, for example, a body which for years resolutely refused to recognise, never mind accept, that a man-made factor influences that which it would manipulate, has designated lengths of Heritage Coast around England's perimeter and declared some inland countryside Areas of Outstanding Natural Beauty. Both types of designation depend upon scenic attributes, upon qualities of landscape which, though defined and specified up to a point, essentially rest in the eyes of the perceiver. Beyond what can be seen by the trained eye, they lie in the cultural tastes of the individuals looking to implement designation. Widely recognised as ultimately a subjective process, such designation results in a management tool the effects of which have been both welcomed and criticised.

Much the same is true of the flagships of this managerial effort, the National Parks, partly inspired by the idea of the American National Parks but like them only in being situated mostly in the west of the country and incorporating low-grade, low-value land. Nevertheless, they represent a considerable national effort to manage a rural heritage, based on the premise that this is best done by picking out bits of the countryside and looking after them in special ways.

The premise can of course be questioned, both in general philosophical terms and in the particulars of what has actually happened in areas designed as 'special' in one way or another. At the one level, has government the right to impose a 'this is different' label not just on a landscape but on the communities who live and work in it? At the other is the proliferation of real-life, white-on-brown labels which now so characterise the specialness of our designated areas: are they the unavoidable price to be paid communally to achieve that ease of access, that general availability, basic to the Countryside Commission's statutory purpose? And, indicative of the deep issues just behind what appear to be common sense moves to protect and manage 'heritage landscape', merely to ask 'Is nothing in our countryside allowed to be personal and secret any longer?' is more likely to provoke charges of élitism than a simple 'yes' or 'no'.

Management here, very conscious to the extent that little of the British landscape is not now contrived, is equally nearly always skirting public controversy. The issues are not so much about its day-to-day practice (though that leads to many a local brouhaha) as the validity of the bases for that practice and its long-term objectives. It was no coincidence that Marion Shoard's radical, anti-proprietorial analysis of the British countryside was called *This Land is Our Land* (1987) and that the 1989 exhibition in The Mall celebrating 150 years of the Royal Agricultural Society was also called 'This Land is Our Land'. One could perhaps be forgiven for suspecting a silent phrase, 'Oh no, it's not' in front of the latter, and detecting in it a slight emphasis on the possessive adjective.

Sidestepping philosophy and questions of ownership, the government has recently become more directly involved in some aspects of land-management as a reaction to a combination of changes in EC agricultural policy, the economics of food production, environmental pressures and the social consequences in the countryside of all three. While these matters take us well beyond the management of the past, in fact some of this direct action has significant management implications for heritage. Probably most important are two developments. One is the implementation of the principle that, instead of payments being made to landowners or tenants for *not* carrying out environmentally damaging operations, they should be paid for implementing environmentally sound husbandry agreed in advance in a management plan. Thus, at the simplest level, instead of a farmer being paid not to break the law by ploughing up a Scheduled Ancient Monument, he is paid under a five-year management agreement to look after the monument in a specified way as part of his occupancy of the land. In a different order of agreement, a whole tract of countryside can likewise be agreed to be managed in a particular way: the Halvergate marshes in Norfolk were the test case where, rather than using government grants to drain the marsh as had been encouraged for previously acceptable agricultural improvement, traditional practice which had created a particular eco-niche was now in effect paid for out of public funds. In other words environmental considerations were deemed more important to the public interest than 'cost-effective' food production was to the individual proprietor in a society with a food surplus.

The second mechanism grew out of that farmer/conservationist clash in the Broads and is more directly linked to a heritage interest. Environmentally Sensitive Areas (ESAs) have been created under Section 18 of the Agriculture Act 1986, following the agreement of the European Community Council to the proposal that member states could pay 'aids' to farmers in suitably designated areas of high conservation value 'to encourage farming practices favourable to the environment' (this, and all other quotes here, are from the Ministry of Agriculture, Fisheries and Food, *Environmentally Sensitive Areas*, 1989). Ten have been defined and are being administered by that former *bête noire* of environmental, and especially archaeological, conservation, the Ministry of Agriculture, Fisheries and Food (MAFF).

Once an ESA has been defined, entry into its provisions is entirely voluntary by local farmers but the cash return from farming in a particular way in an age of sharply declining farm income is, under a management agreement, attractive in some cases. In principle, an ESA seems a miracle of creative practicality from a conservation point of view, covering as it does virtually all aspects of the environment, man-made as well as natural. An agreement can include, for example, the maintenance of redundant farm buildings and anachronistic field walls, both crucial visual elements of 'old landscapes' quite apart from their scientific interest in areas such as the Yorkshire Dales. So, along with the creation of features such as ponds and the planting of new copses, agreement between farmer and MAFF in an ESA should be emphasising the positive side of landscape management rather than just propping up the old.

Clearly there is an element in such devices of trying to control through management the appearance of a landscape. 'Oldness', expressed in phrases such as 'traditional landscape', is almost inevitably one of the elements present in such a maintained appearance and nowadays a great deal of thought goes into achieving just such an effect. Often this reaches no higher an intellectual level than consciously preserving individually-known and obvious structures like a windmill or a tithe barn. The concept has developed, however, of 'the historic landscape' and even of 'ancient landscapes', consisting not just of all such structures but of all the other elements, man-made or natural, which have been in place for some time.

These could include, for example, ruinous walls defining now disused lanes, once vital for local communication; or a hedge-line, just another edge along a field at one level of perception but actually following the boundary perambulation described in a tenth-century Anglo-Saxon charter as established at another level of perception by a fairly elementary piece of documentary and fieldwork research. In other words, a minor revelation occurs, converting a mere hedge into a permanent feature in the landscape for a thousand and more years. The process of defining these is relatively simple and matter-of-fact; the difficulty comes in judging for management purposes the weight of the enhanced value the hedge has thereby acquired.

The most ordinary-looking elements in a landscape can become significant, and therefore valuable, in this perception: not just a patch of old woodland, for example, but its contents and its very shape; not just a group of still-used fields but their size, shape and boundaries; not just a disregarded area of useless scrubland but its disturbed surface and its location in relation to the village. In addition to such visible features, however ordinary, any landscape is full too of its 'invisibles', its former settlements, religious places, fields and cemeteries which have been erased and eroded, buried and built upon, over five or more millennia of continual occupancy in many parts of Britain. While one difficulty lies in simply putting this dynamic concept across to land-managers, even more difficult is explaining the idea that very often 'significance' lies not in the feature itself but in its relationships across space and through time with other phenomena, the nature and even location of which is often uncertain at the moment.

Such dimensions pose a considerable management problem. They require, for one thing, a much higher level of intellectual awareness and sympathy than has been the norm in planning circles; they demand a high level of awareness and skill among the consultancy agencies now blossoming to meet the needs of Environmental Impact Assessments. But in a sense that is not the real problem: the huge challenge, especially when this concept of 'the historic environment' is grasped, is how to manage the landscape by taking everything knowledgeably and sympathetically into account (of which heritage matters are only a part) and yet still produce a landscape, an environment, *which actually works*. 'Managing the past' can mean giving a priority on occasion to our inheritance over and above the interests of our daily bread-winning; but we cannot set everything aside, nor is fossilising our countryside the answer to conservation needs, never mind all the other needs of society.

'Heritage management' is fast developing as a speciality, with several systematic courses at various institutions of higher education now available. The need is for people not simply trained in running commodified and often invented pastiches of pastness as a branch of the leisure industry but able to deal intelligently, sympathetically and skilfully with an assortment of the matters touched on here. Such professional competence must stem from an appreciation of perceived parts of 'real pasts' as communal resources. Sympathy with such a point of view is, however, not enough, though it is the essential first base to reach. Clever adjustment of resources and pragmatism are also required. Given that sympathy, for example in the Forestry Commission, the sheer amount of archaeology now recognised in some woodlands can nevertheless make for severe problems in continuing to manage the land by well-tried professional forestry methods for legitimate silvicultural purposes. The past in its archaeological form is, after all, often crowding in on land already full of other management constraints ranging from ecological to commercial. Ultimately the success or otherwise of managing the past out of doors in this sense will lie in its ability to cope, not just with the known features as single spies, but with the past anonymous battalions and all the other 'occupiers' that share our landscapes with us; and to do so within the normal precepts and practices of land-use management.

All the past received by the present is filtered to some extent: pastness does not come in a pure essence. The rest of us receive what someone else has decided should be our fare. But beyond this core of consciously managed past, only a small nucleus of what is available, a huge grey area of pastnesses also come through to us as the result of unconscious biases, a myriad of single decisions, a sense in society of what sorts of past it wants on its menu today. These are both reflected in, and to some extent created by, the uses made of the past at any one time.

Just *using* the past, often by simply appealing to it, seemed to come almost as second nature in the Britain of the 1980s, Patrick White's 'Old Country'. It is difficult to envisage things changing in this respect in the 1990s for surely they too will have their fair share of gut appeals to the past. One late-1980s incident, for example, is likely to be of a recurring type: it was concerned at the practical level with the long-running saga of access to land, in this case a common. The issue is likely to become a major one – again – in the run-up to the end of the century.

One of those usually anonymous epitomes of 'the common man', Brian Wright 'tries to keep open an ancient right of way by slashing a path through the crops ...' in a field on Sonning Common, Oxfordshire. It was Enclosed as recently as 1816, only 174 years ago, a mere flick of a bucolic eyelid ago in an old countryside. When the press (O, 1 July) pinpointed his cut and thrust argument, and Patrick Anstee's similar problem about grazing his cattle on Kingwood Common in the same county, time was running up to an expected ministerial announcement about commons in the autumn. This would respond to the remarkably homogeneous report of the Common Land Forum in 1988. Anstee's commoners' rights, naturally enjoyed by his forebears for generations, were not registered by 1970 (Commons Registration Act) and therefore did not legally exist. His situation is common: 'only one-fifth of common land in England and Wales ... is subject to a legal right of access'. In other words, four-fifths of common land are not common at all, not even to individuals with historic user rights, never mind the public.

Journalistic technique shows somewhat at the seams as the predictable heritage-speak quote followed: 'Common land, like our footpaths, is a vital part of our national heritage ...' (spokesperson for the Open Spaces Society). An implication of that might be, since common land is part of heritage and we do not legally own the former, that we do not own our heritage either; but the interest here is essentially the appeal to the past over the head of mere legislation, quite recent legislation too compared to other fields. The Wright sort of rough stuff follows from the real or imagined priority, depending on your point of view, afforded by the sanctity of the past: villagers in Nuffield 'have incurred the wrath of Huntercombe Golf Club, which owns the common there, by claiming that the "privilege of playing games" on the common includes golf – making a mockery of the club's £300-a-year membership fee'. Nice point; but when was golf invented? Before or after 'ancient' times?

Golf, of course, is a game which occupies quite large stretches of country-side. It is also a very traditional game, or so it would like others to think. It now has its own British Golf Museum at – where else? – St Andrews, central shrine of an army of devotees. It is also a very heritage-sensitive game, partly because of the space it exclusively occupies and partly because of the way in which the high membership fees of its private clubs perpetuate élitist attitudes and class-distinctions. Substitute race for class, and colour for class-difference, and Nuffield with its land claim of indigenous people against the intruder bore a marked similarity to synchronous problems over a golf-course near Ottawa. But of course we don't have nasty incidents like that in England; after all, we don't have any 'natives' for are we not all 'native'? It is part of our communal heritage that we continue to delude ourselves on that score, not least in the way that we use the past.

Using the past 9

One of the numerous 'past' books to appear in 1990 was called *The Pleasures of the Past*. The author, David Cannadine, remarked in his preface, dated 13 September 1988, that '... behind all this lies the particular and pervasive climate of opinion current in Thatcher's England and Reagan's America, which has deeply influenced both the type and the content of British history produced during the present 1980s decade'.

He realised, of course, that to an extent his own book reflected the accuracy of his observation: he, as with the author of this book, was a participant in the use of the past as well as an observer of some of those uses. One of the interesting facets of the contemporary past will be the degree, in post-Reagan, post-Thatcher times, to which it reflects any particular climate of the 1990s. It may well indeed, as society uses it in changed circumstances, contribute significantly to that climate; for, as another historian, J. H. Plumb, observed in the introduction to his book *The Death of the Past*, 'The more literate and sophisticated the society becomes, the more complex and powerful become the uses to which the past is put.' And that was in 1969, allowing us to ponder on the correctness of *his* observation in *our* time. Given the unlikelihood of our society becoming less sophisticated in the 1990s, we may well wonder about the 'more complex and powerful' uses to which the past will be put during the decade of the 1990s.

Contemporary use of the past goes much further than just making use of it for, say, a display of old photographs in the village hall or as a visual, physically preserved structure in the landscape. This latter use is, after all, characteristically as a mere convenience, a facility, often in ignorance of its significance as something old, a survival, let alone of its scientific or cultural value. A whole range of further human activity consciously seeks to use all sorts of manifestations of 'pastness', knowing them to be old. Here we look first at some of those which are basically altruistic, neutral or even benign.

Past workings

People have studied the past in Europe since at least Classical times. Academic scholarship continues to be one of the more altruistic uses to which it is put. Of course, such activity generates work and paid jobs; the cynic could well argue that it has now generated a self-interested, self-perpetuating élite. The contemporary, professional world of historical study in the widest sense was, however, formerly the preserve of the amateur in the proper sense of the word, that is 'one who is fond of'; and fortunately that remains a strong motivation in the field. Professionalism, both in the sense of widely-recognised, effective standards and a structure of paid posts, is a relatively recent phenomenon in the use of the past. The growth in the number of museums and universities over the last century has clearly been a major factor, supplemented by the increasing involvement of central and local government in the care and use of the past (Pl. 31).

The range of this professional establishment is now from highly-paid Civil Servants and Directors of various national 'heritage' organisations, at salaries of *c.* £55,000 a year and more, to a temporary museum cataloguer on perhaps *c.* £6,000 a year, or a post-graduate student in a Department of Archaeology struggling to make ends meet on a British Academy grant of *c.* £3,000 a year. Whatever the material benefits (or otherwise) to the practitioners of the past, their motivation by and large has to be basically altruistic and well-intentioned. A life devoted to study of the past is pretty pointless without a strong belief in its validity as a field of scholarship for its own sake. 'Public benefit' arising from such study may well be irrelevant to the purist scholar but, in practice, not least because the source of funding for the activity is in most cases public money, the development of professionalism, exemplified in museum and archaeological codes of conduct, now specifically includes that as a responsibility. Scholarship, and the administration of various types of past at best based upon it, must count as one of the prime users of the past, a use now requiring (or at least involving) many thousands of paid staff.

Another highly-motivated use is, like scholarship, partly of the primary past in the form of original evidence in field and museum; but it also stems from the results of scholarship and in that sense is a consumer of secondary pastness. The role of the past in education is a highly controversial subject, and not just in Britain, as contemporary societies approach the twenty-first century pondering their future and consequently uncertain of the role of their pasts. 'White' Australia, for example, is not entirely unambiguous in its attitude to the pre-colonial past of the continent, and the Biblically fundamentalist interpretation of history is not entirely without its supporters in the USA. In Britain, very few adults seem to have enjoyed their history at school; yet an impression is that among the small minority who did so, a high proportion of them take an abiding interest through life. This may frequently encompass a professional career based on it, perhaps as a schoolteacher or in museums, or an active hobby, perhaps in a local archaeological society. Such commitment seems often to have been triggered by one individual, a gifted schoolteacher perhaps (Pl. 32) or an enthusiastic local historian free with his or her time and the results of a lifetime's accumulated information.

If such surmise is correct, it is a most extraordinary thing that popular expression of an interest in pastness has become such a feature of the later twentieth century. Perhaps that is to identify it at too high an intellectual level; the impulse may be no more than a curiosity, no more cerebral than a need to fill in time with the trimmings of an 'experience', equivalent to a wander along the covered ways of some huge shopping mall. Interest or curiosity, it clearly does not stem from formal education in school, and its motors must be sought elsewhere. Popular school education for over a century has, nevertheless, been based in part on the assumption that history was an integral part of it, not perhaps quite as basic as the three Rs but second only to them. This view was rather confirmed in January 1991 by the judgement of the Secretary of State for Education on the place of history in the new Schools National Curriculum: bowing to teacher pressure about the overcrowding of the timetable, he accepted that history should not be compulsory throughout secondary schooling. A few days later he drew a distinction between 'history' and 'current affairs', stopping the former in the 1960s. Whatever the validity or otherwise of this very nice point, it cannot be regarded kindly in a book potentially made officially redundant before it reaches the press precisely because it is largely based on the premise that the past exists *primarily* as current affairs.

Looking at Victorian school books now, however, and that includes some still in the classroom, one somehow doubts whether the motivation to teach it ever has been of a disinterested 'history for history's sake' school of thought. 'History' last century, for example, was unquestioningly a good thing, it seems, primarily because it showed that Britain, and especially England, was a very good thing indeed, i.e. for the rest of the world, as viewed from Britain. This imperialistic view of the past was punctured two generations ago by two body blows, the straight scholastic left of Butterfield's *Whig Interpretation of History* (1931) and the right hook of ridicule in one of the most brilliant historical satires ever written, Sellars's and Yeatman's *1066 and All That* (1930). Of the former's date of publication, Plumb wrote (*op cit.*, p. 42) '... 1931, a most appropriate date, for this year, more than any other, proclaimed the coming dissolution of the British Empire'.

Past workings

The equivalent date in archaeology was 1966 when Grahame Clark's article, 'The invasion hypothesis in British archaeology' (*Antiquity* 40, 172–89) articulated increasing dissatisfaction with the existing model of a long-term British past 'explained' largely in terms of change induced by the arrival of foreigners, i.e. Britain's view of her world role in reverse. That this knock on the archaeological interpretative kaleidoscope came a full generation after Butterfield says much for the profound influence, from General Roy through General Pitt-Rivers to Brigadier Mortimer Wheeler, of militaristic attitudes on archaeology in and of Britain.

Nevertheless, even archaeology's submission to the winds of change was twenty-five years ago now and yet, amazingly but drawing on deep reserves of populist and political resistance to a post-imperial view of the past, gung-ho history persisted. Through the popular books of historians such as Churchill and Bryant and throughout the patchwork phase of history teaching in the 1960s and 1970s, it bumbled along, remote from the cutting edge of historical thought and research but echoed in many a novel and TV programme. Many, including quite obviously some politicians, did not therefore realise that its day had passed. Equally, however, to the surprise of many others, it re-emerged in the 1980s as a major claimant in the national debate about what sort of history society wanted its minors to imbibe (disregarding for present purposes the interesting Thatcherian *diktat* that synchronously denied the existence of 'society'). Indeed, some of the proponents of what seemed at times to be nationalistic rather than merely national history seemed somewhat baffled, not to say exasperated, by the realisation that there could be any other sort of history; and advocates of those other sorts, economic and social, local and global, for example, soon found to *their* surprise that they stood pretty close to being branded 'unpatriotic'. Quite what 'patriotism' has to do with a supposedly disinterested quest for understanding of the past through scholarship is a moot point. Clearly, however, 'nation-state history' can become a vexed question when, as is frequently the case, politicians sense a threat to, not so much the state itself, but rather to their hegemony over it. 'All rulers', observed Plumb of ancient times, 'needed an interpretation of the past to justify the authority of their government', a generalisation which would seem to be one of the perhaps few genuine lessons history can teach.

Education, then, incorporating an element of history, inevitably raises questions of 'What history?' Any answer in practice is as much to do with the politics of the day as with absolutes of scholarship or current educational theory. A *place* for history in the core curriculum of the British state educational system has now been confirmed so, although that place is not so central or large as many would have wished, attention can now turn to the working-out in the schools of the content of the curriculum itself. The use of the past in practical terms can be crucial, not just to the mindset formulated by the pupils during a minimum nine years of exposure but also to the nature and shape of 'schools history' as it actually emerges.

Teaching demand will, for example, lead to the writing of particular textbooks and the non-writing of others. Already, to quote but one example among many interests which submitted evidence to the National History Working Group, the Council for British Archaeology expressed disappointment that ' "prehistory", which comprises over 90 per cent of the past (and is a popular area of study in the primary school) is so sparsely represented, and vaguely defined in the Working Group's Interim Report'. With marked restraint, and perhaps a hint of sarcasm, it continued: 'Presumably the phrases "Ancient Times" and "Ancient World" encapsulate "prehistory". We feel that these phrases should be defined more precisely.' Quite. This particular CBA evidence also seized very positively on a use of history firmly recommended by the Report: 'a concern for the environment and its inheritance from the past requires an understanding of, and respect for, that inheritance encouraged by the study of History.' The CBA sought to link this with a Thematic Study Unit, 'Conserving our inheritance: the use of the past in the present and future'.

This sort of development would have been conceptually impossible twenty years ago, and is probably only possible at all now through the agency of an imposed national curriculum. Whatever one may think of the merits of such an agency, the thrust in this example towards environmental awareness and stewardship would presumably command general contemporary assent. It certainly seems highly desirable in a world at last seized of the concepts of finite resources and the interdependence of people and environment. Nevertheless, the educational implementation of such concepts in Study Units like the one instanced above, in that case as a result of a well-considered and *conscious* decision about policy, will be as much a manipulation of history for present purposes as were the partly *unconscious* assumptions about the desirability of British imperialism in the teaching of history a century ago.

Now, one of the most dangerous varieties of history, much favoured in educational and entertainment circles, is that called 'living history'. Feelings, as elsewhere on the interface of past and present, can run high on the subject. It is, however, much relished by consumers with big appetites for pasts. Such gourmandising undoubtedly meets a demand, as undoubtedly do *The Sun* and fast-food take-aways; but they at least exist. 'Living history' is an impossible concept; therefore any attempt to realise it is bound to produce a fraud. So much for the absolute; in practice, like so much else, it all depends on motivation and honesty.

Past workings

With some undergraduate students I recently went back to 'school' in the 'Victorian' classroom constructed for the delectation of the tourist trade at Wigan Pier. The 'teacher' was a professional actor in period dress. For me, it proved a terrifying experience, subsequently rationalised. As a five-year-old starting my education in a two-class, all-age village school deep in feudal Oxfordshire in the early 1940s, I had unknowingly just glimpsed the tail-end of a particular educational tradition; and it was not just that I had been taught to write with chalk on a slate or to chant my times tables in petrified unison. Anyway, as a result now, this middle-aged adult unintentionally sniggered in an inadvertent release of tension as the flood, not just of memories but of long-forgotten *emotions*, especially fear, overwhelmed him. I was publicly chastised by 'teacher' for being naughty. *My* students of course thought this highly amusing but, unlike the actor acting or them being entertained, I was neither acting nor amused. Not one of them had experienced the reality in the past that my past was evoking and, however well a simulated reality was being created at that moment, for all of them the episode was but make-believe and only make-believe. The actor stopped acting when his shift was over; the 'class' walked out and consumed some other bits of a pre-selected past. They had seen and heard and participated but had not emoted. But for me it was all too *real*: ancestral voices indeed, a professor reduced to an innocent, guilt-ridden little boy of fifty years ago. My emotions triggered, I had once again felt what it was actually like to be a nothing in a no-win situation dominated by an all-powerful, all-seeing and all-hearing grown-up autocrat.

As a matter of fact, entering the 'show' with a video-camera very obviously around my neck, I had ostentatiously put it in the desk, on the spur of the moment surreptitiously switching it on as I closed the lid. Now that really was naughty. I left with a racing pulse, twenty minutes of used, blank film and a perfect sound recording of the whole episode. Whose past is it anyway?

The point of the story is not, however, to record the recorded recapture of my past but to distinguish between 'feeling' and acting the past. It is all too easy to dress up as a Roman soldier or a medieval knight: with a bit of care, the clothes can be reasonably accurate simulations, as far as we know, of what such people would have worn. In the process of making and dressing, some idea of historical research and some experience of practical problems such as sewing coarse cloth can be imparted to pupils by serious teachers. Further use of the past is then a logical step: to form up as Roman soldiers in marching order or to process round the ruins of an abbey according to well-documented monkish practice, for example. That too is legitimate and it can be, provided it is properly done, educationally stimulating. It is, however, concerned only with the physicalities of a series of pasts in the present. It is when the organiser, teacher or re-enactment specialist fails to stress that participants' feelings cannot be 'historical' that the method gets out of hand; worse if such a person encourages those involved 'to feel what it was like to be a medieval monk'.

No one today can possibly know what it was actually like to be a medieval monk: even if our historical record was perfect, five hundred years of subsequent acculturation would prevent any of us achieving anything like verisimilitude. It is self-delusion to think otherwise; but the real danger is that, aided by appropriate clothes and a suitable setting, it is only too easy to move from the stimulation of the imagination affording us some idea of what certain aspects of the past might have been like to actually believing that what we have experienced is like what it was. Such created pasts may be convincing, which is why they are so pernicious; but they can never actually be realistic, genuine re-creations of what once was, for the simple reason that *we* are different.

This presents a basic difficulty for museums, that form of human activity among the most conspicuous users of the past. 'What an outrageous remark' cry the museum professionals and their legions of friends throughout the land. 'Museums preserve and care for the past, making it available to all; they are not mere users.' True; but their stock-in-trade does rather tend to be of the past and it is certainly what most of them exist to collect, look after and present. So generically they are users, in the best possible sense of course, and occasionally they might even make an appeal to the past in justifying themselves. That should not, however, be necessary, for to collect 'curios' seems a fairly basic thing for civilised society to do and to bring them into the public arena seems a praiseworthy objective. It is a curious paradox then that the word 'museum' has generally come, outside museological circles, to be a term of denigration. Was it not the former Prime Minister of the United Kingdom herself who declared that she did not want to preside over a 'museum society'?

Part of the problem, disregarding the historical lack of resources and talent, is precisely that people are different now from then, whenever the 'then' was; so interpretation, the repackaging of things and images from the past for meaningful contemporary contemplation, is fundamental to the museums' role. It is one in which they have signally failed in the twentieth century. Until recently, museology ignored sociology and it is now, literally, paying the price.

The reasons for this awareness-gap are doubtless complex and little understood. A crude generalisation might be that the museum world has simply failed to keep pace with the needs and aspirations of a rapidly changing society; perhaps it has tended towards the cardinal sin of thereby making itself sociologically irrelevant. This would mirror the fact that less than 10 per cent of the population ever go inside museums and, put the other way round, that a high proportion of non-visitors is made up of the less privileged members of society, such as those dependent on public transport, physically handicapped or receiving some form of social security. This would accord with the other side of the same coin, museums' popular image of élitism, the privileged sanctuary of dull scholars both on the staff and visiting to poke around in dusty boxes. Clichés, no doubt, but just ask anyone in the street: the chances are that he or she would not even know there is a museum locally, let alone where it is.

The 1980s, however, have seen great changes, and no informed person can deny that the museum world has tried, and continues to try, to put its houses in order. Again, reasons are difficult to define but undoubtedly rising professional standards and more alert leadership have helped. Probably the most significant factor, however, has been external threat in the form of competing 'museums'. Not all such creations are museums in the traditional sense – Wigan Pier does not have responsibility for a large scholarly collection accumulated over a century of endeavour, for example – but, whether they are called 'heritage centre' or give a twist to the accepted meaning of 'museum', the critical point is that they are jumping up and down competing for people's attention, time and disposable income.

Those very people include those predisposed by acculturation and aspiration to go to museums anyway; but they also embrace, beyond this traditional clientele, the untapped potential audience the curator has long suspected was there but knew not how to approach. Establishments such as the North of England Museum, Beamish, and Ironbridge with Blists Hill have tapped into near-pasts at or only just beyond the limits of personal memory, thereby successfully edging into this further customer band. The Jorvik Viking Centre has also done so, not through the relatively easy appeal of recent pasts but through superb marketing and presentation of a popularly little-known past arranged, like burgers, in a convenient, instant and easily assimilable form. Given the research-based academic integrity of the product, it is difficult to resist the argument of its creators that Jorvik is good, popular education. Many critics have failed to distinguish clearly between that objective and the overtly Disney-inspired mechanism designed to achieve it. That distinction is now manifest in the demonstration by the Archaeological Resource Centre, York, of another format to achieve an educational objective (Pl. 33). The Centre also illustrates innovatively an appropriate use for a redundant church.

The influence of the Jorvik style is meanwhile everywhere apparent, in museums and across a range of other past-users. An emphasis on exciting, visually-led, vocabularily-simple presentation, on making things and stories accessible, involves, however, an element of glitz. At 'The Tales of Robin Hood', Nottingham, 'hard history' is posted all over the walls while fantasy, descending into the crude ghost train thrills of skulls and skeletons along the route of your suspended time capsule through the 'magical forest', emerges triumphant at the end of your journey in a Ruritanian scene of Robin *in excelsis*. 'Oops', said the attendant as my capsule was jerked back to today after a flattering false start on the sound track, 'wrong language'.

Predictably in a market-led economy, but unfortunately for the integrity of several pasts, some would-be copycats have gone for 'the experience' alone, forgetting or not realising that behind Jorvik, and indeed 'Robin Hood', is academic substance. The ambivalence of contemporary use of the past, however, is that such a value judgement has to be seen as stemming from an assumption of scholarly propriety. That is not necessarily of unquestioned priority in an age when neither the marketeer nor the consumer need be particularly bothered by concepts of integrity or details of accuracy. 'Feel the width of the prehistoric hut/Roman forum/medieval street, never mind the quality' is an attitude not only easy to adopt but also one apparently acceptable in a heritage-consuming society at the point where use of the past elides into its exploitation (Pl. 34). Not that availability alone is sufficient: 'security' is another important ingredient in the commodity. 'Learn of their life and working conditions', the Black Country Museum exhorts would-be visitors to its coal miners, 'without worrying about the dangers they would have faced.' Don't just be safe: *feel* safe, for the past is a dangerous country.

It is easy enough to mock at this 'olde-worlde' syndrome, but from it stem many other uses of the past today. Sport, for example, is hooked on its numerous pasts to a perhaps surprising extent, golf being by no means exceptional in harping on its history or peddling its traditions. Indeed, as more and more sport goes commercial, so the tendency increases to look back to the good old days of the amateur and to use that past and its virtues as promotional material in the contemporary, competitive world of sponsorship, TV deals and professionalism. Rugby Union Football, poised uncomfortably on the very edge of that world, has actively used 1990 to celebrate the centenary of the Barbarians RFC, extolling those very virtues of the traditional amateur approach: 'We play hard and we play to win but it is the manner of our playing, not the result, that really matters,' as one of its ex-internationals explained on television. A competition to publicise the forthcoming World Cup, to be staged in Britain in 1991, required entrants to design a mascot with 'a strong "local" identity perhaps taken from [a county's] history or heritage . . .'.

Cricket is an even more outstanding and complex example. How it survives at the level of superb individual excellence of Test match standard is a miracle; though, at one level of explanation, it does so simply because it invented a debased, populist version of itself as crowd-puller and commercial-deal fodder. Another facet is that, though limited in its global incidence, it has carried through from its origins a loyal and devoted following at club level which would continue whether or not the experts played Test and inter-state or county cricket. Its very essence of pastness, of old fogeyness, is too a great strength; and it plays to it.

This may be little comfort to the worthy, helmetless club batsman facing a barrage of maybe second generation but distinctly Caribbean bouncers on a dusty park pitch of a Saturday afternoon, but a sport has much on its side which can summon up from the past great heroes, memorable moments of physical and aesthetic climax, and satisfying images of oil-stained bats and musky, manly dressing rooms. It is also fantastically sexy, though that has more to do with others' perceptions derived from their pasts than with the game itself. Nevertheless, it is a characteristic now seized on by manufacturers and advertisers: a combination of antique virtues, sexual symbolism and the individual hero is difficult to resist. And cricket, like most sport in Britain, is fundamentally conservative, its participants overwhelmingly right-wing in political terms: hence the success of the repeated siren-calls from South Africa. Sport therefore has a 'hidden' use as another sort of spectator-sport worldwide. We watch as it struggles with its pasts in the present: adjusting to contemporary realities, it provides memories and a surrogate for reality (Pl. 35).

The essential competitiveness of sport is also present more directly in relation to pastness in other fields. Archaeologists, for example, compete with one another every two years in the British Archaeological Awards, the supreme champion, as it were, making off with the Silver Trowel. Essentially, of course, the event is a PR exercise, primarily to encourage good practice by users of archaeology rather than archaeologists themselves. It affords the opportunity to give public acknowledgement to developers and corporations who have done the right thing archaeologically, to sponsors of projects and to publishers of archaeological works; and certainly the 'winners' seem to derive pleasure and good publicity from the awards. The whole idea of such competition, and especially the somewhat artificial nature of the award-giving occasion, was and is anathema to some, especially to some archaeologists. The fact is, nevertheless, that in a competitive world archaeology has shown that it can modestly compete for attention in terms that that world understands yet without descending to either the banality of, for example, 'Sports Personality of the Year' or the mega-hype of some even greater non-events.

The past is also used by others in competition. The Forestry Commission, for example, was awarded at the end of 1990 the Alan Morshead Award for its management of archaeological sites on its estate in the Dartmoor National Park. Precisely because it will raise an eyebrow or two in the archaeological world, the award will not do that organisation any harm at all. Perhaps less disinterestedly, another example was provided by the Crown Berger Colouring our Lives Awards (in association with the Design Council) 'for those who shape the way we live'. Along with such as 'Fashion in the Home' and 'The Shopping Experience', a 'Conserving Our Heritage' category embraced a field similar to that in another competition already noted (above p. 59). In similar competitive vein, but embracing the less tangible, countless opportunities exist to win something, via a local newspaper for example, by supplying a memory of life in a now-demolished neighbourhood or some personal war-time anecdote. This sort of use of various pasts can supply good, free copy, however trivial or maudlin, helping to sell the paper; and, incidentally, beyond the immediate motivation, it may be putting on permanent record something useful for the future local historian. Curiously, in another of those para-doxes characteristic of our relationships with pastness, it is the immediate mundane past which in some ways is most at risk of oblivion. Its use for present delectation is most definitely to be encouraged for academic reasons alone, and never mind the nostalgia.

Nostalgia, nevertheless, is one of the most powerful motives for con-temporary uses of the past. Some may regret the motive for all sorts of rational reasons but that will not diminish by one the huge TV audiences for 'Those were the Days'-type programmes of Victorian and Edwardian music halls (dressing-up *à l'époque* obligatory of course). The autumn 1990 programme for 'The Good Old Days of Music Hall' at the World Famous City Varieties, Leeds, offered a prize for 'the best dressed party!!' while splurging its alliterative come-ons across five columns of 'Nenuphar Nubility in Essential Femininity' (of the Beverley Sisters!) and the like. Simultaneously television desperately quested its next great success in period costume drama of the 'Brideshead Saga' genre. Nor will it reduce a million obsessions with collecting things from railwayana, like the man with a station lay-out including tall signals in his small suburban garden, to miniatures and matchbox labels, cheese-presses and cigarette packages, treen and trade-cards, stevengraphs and decorated toleware.

These and many other collectables in various media are now themselves mass-reproduced for sale in a characteristic downmarket spiral but the genuine articles are earnestly discussed in, for example, Mackay's *Collecting Local History*, the *entrée* like so many specialist magazines to another world. It is one where, as in treasure-hunting with metal-detectors, collecting for collecting's sake seems dominant. It is, however, also a world of great expertises, where the anonymity of mundane life, perhaps as an insurance clerk or a professor, can be cast aside in metamorphosis as spare-time world expert in some obscure byway of non-academia. Examples might be in a branch of button or badge collecting, notaphily, deltiology or labology. Wright's *Collecting Volunteer Militaria* (1974), Ernest Quarmby's *Banknotes and Banking in the Isle of Man, 1788–1970* (1971), Valerie Monahan's *Collecting Postcards in Colour, 1914–1930* (1980) and Keith W. Osborne's somewhat less modest *The International Book of Beer Labels, Mats and Coasters* (1979) indicate the scope of this infrastructure to the global world of scholarship; while the expected note of ambivalence is struck by Rickards's title, *This is Ephemera: Collecting Printed Throwaways* (1978). Sounds a bit like the art of the impossible exercised on the inconceivable, but then, what is the technique of archaeology at base but the collecting of 'throwaways'?

Monetary worth has now come to enhance or impair, depending on the point of view, the pleasure of many such collections. This development is witnessed by journalistic helpfulness of the sort quoted above (p. 54) and books such as Douglas's *Successful Investing in Stamps and Banknotes...* (1975) and Baynton-Williams's *Investing in Maps* (1969). With such books, and the entry into this demesne of collectors primarily there for financial reasons, we are close to the other, exploitive world of Sotheby's *Guide: Antiques and their prices worldwide* (Chapter 11). But in the relatively harmless users' world, real value remains personal, collecting for their own sake objects both redundant and no longer manufactured. Often they speak, maybe in a small, quiet voice, of craftsmanship, even of a different and better scale of moral and social values; and, though such meaning may be read into them rather than be explicit, they characteristically provide for hassled lives little oases of calm and contemplation in their 'other-ageness', in their seeming permanence as a unique collection fashioned in a personal image.

Mackay argues that, in addition, 'the popular hobby of collecting can become far more interesting and rewarding when linked with the study of British local history'. 'Instead of collecting certain subjects ... to the exclusion of all else, how much more fascinating to integrate the different media to develop the story of one locality.' That is doubtless true, and the same argument has been used both to justify treasure-hunting and to raise its status. Such a development may be desirable, for social and academic reasons for example, but it will not necessarily appeal to the collector pure and simple nor need it do so. Collecting *per se* is sufficient unto itself, needing no further justification in the mind of the true collector. That is fine, a natural use of the past affording great personal satisfaction, of sociological rather than scholarly significance if significant at all; but the trouble is that such innocent self-indulgence can spill over into anti-social consequences the moment private satisfaction moves on to an exploitive strategy.

10 | *Touring the past*

The razor edge between use and exploitation is walked in other fields relating to the past. Nowhere is this more so than with the tourist industry. Whichever side of the edge it comes down, behind its economic vagaries lie, especially in terms of its relations with pastness as a resource, a range of philosophical issues which perhaps do not always feature in its own considerations of its practical problems. Should tourism, for example, be encouraged? At one level and in many circumstances, the answer is clearly 'yes'; but an ever-growing tourist industry is not inevitably an unmixed blessing and, even in those circumstances where its further development is apparently desirable, the case for an obvious 'yes' will usually be less overwhelming on deeper consideration.

A very fine line indeed exists between, on the one hand, letting people know of the attractions of a place in the hope that they will visit it and, on the other, aggressively marketing those attractions using hyperbole and an economy with the truth. Those are extremes either side of a wide grey area difficult to avoid impinging upon and characteristically occupied by the tourist industry.

It includes, nevertheless, what might be called 'polite tourism'. The National Trust, in existence to conserve 'places of historic interest or natural beauty', uses the past it looks after in a deceptively well-mannered way in the form of its annual *Handbook: A guide for members and visitors*. Though its members do not pay for entry, all are potential customers of the tea-rooms and shops; but such attractions, like the historic ones of the properties, are merely listed and described, not extolled. Information is made available; whether and how it is used is up to the reader, in practice as much the entry-paying non-member as the member.

This low-key approach is deceptive in the sense that attracting visitors is a matter of cut-throat competition, for many more attractions are now available clamouring for the expenditure of individuals' leisure time; and many tend to shout their wares and whereabouts. Though the Trust knows how and when to compete in like manner as appropriate, in general its laid-back approach works well enough in attracting its on the whole fairly discerning potential clientele. Indeed, some properties, in the interests of their conservation, need to be protected from too many visitors so techniques of de-advertisement have to be devised. Possibly because many visitors to NT country houses, gardens and the like are unconsciously seeking a sense of familiarity, security, even cosiness, rather than intellectual rigour or brash commercialism, the Trust is virtually alone in appearing able to afford such coolness in its use of the past.

Uses by others tend to be graded upwards from the NT level in terms of temperature. The following observations are based on much visiting and a fairly casual collection of freely available information leaflets and promotional pamphlets removed in recent months from hotel lobbies, information centres and other places where tourists gather. How is the past used for them?

Taking Scotland as an example, the answer is 'ubiquitously'. The Scottish Highlands and Islands tourist leaflet enjoins you in Argyll and the Isles to 'visit pre-historic standing stones; go cruising in waters saints and Vikings have sailed'; in the Heart (what else?) of the Highlands it offers 'Britain's oldest monster, Nessie' (then, indiscriminately changing gear to hype, 'she may also be the shyest but could well pop out to see you': cf. the journalistic come-on to Cheddar Man (above p. 36) and 'the sites of ancient battlefields'. In the Northern Highlands and Islands 'In the course of a day you can come across ... stone-age remains and magnificent castles ... And at the end ... you can frequently enjoy a ceilidh ... into the wee small hours' (nae doot). While doubtless too 'You'll be amazed at what goes on here after sunrise' if you 'Take the trail to Angus' invented by the Angus and Scottish Tourist Boards, you must contain your disappointment that 'Despite evidence of previous civilisations in Angus the main towns date from early 12th and 13th century'. Nevertheless, they variously contain an 'historic Abbey', a Signal Tower Museum, a Cathedral and Round Tower, the Caledonian Railway Station, 'now revived and the hub for steam and other train enthusiasts', and 'a lively early history linked with Scottish Royals and raiding rebels' at Forfar which 'unfortunately lost its Castle in one such foray'; and so on. Mainly descriptive, hoping to attract by stressing the interest rather than hitting the reader with exaggeration; but tourist-speak nevertheless.

Similarly quite low-key in their use of local pasts are many other information leaflets about Scotland. The Clyde Valley may not be everyone's first thought as a holiday location and hence presumably its *Handbook for a Happy Holiday*. This picks out eight 'Major Attractions' and, despite the rival claims of swimming pools, a trout and deer farm, golf courses, shopping and a racecourse, all are 'historic'. They are: Bothwell Castle, 'the finest surviving 13th Century castle in Scotland'; the David Livingstone Centre, 'Birthplace of the famous missionary/explorer' with an exciting and lively exhibition of his life story, a social history museum and Africa Pavilion; Strathclyde Park where you can visit 'the excavated Roman bath-house, and the Mausoleum of the Dukes of Hamilton, famous for its echo'; Chatelherault, 'Former hunting lodge of Dukes of Hamilton designed by William Adam in 1732' (where the quality of presentation fails to match the essential quality of the restored architecture); Craignethan Castle, Sir Walter Scott's 'Tillietudlem Castle', fifteenth-century home to the Hamiltons and 'reputedly haunted by a headless Mary Queen of Scots'; the Falls of Clyde, natural but enhanced by having been 'visited by Dickens and Wordsworth and painted by Turner'; New Lanark, 'A unique industrial village established by David Dale in 1785 and the site of Robert Owen's radical social and educational experiments ... Nominated as a World Heritage Site' (which gives out confused and confusing messages to the visitor); and Biggar's Museums, the Gladstone Court Museum with its Victorian Street, Greenhill Covenanter's House, an original seventeenth-century farmhouse with 'relics of Covenanting times', and Moat Park Heritage Centre with 'fascinating local history'.

Pastness is clearly of considerable importance here in trying to make the area attractive, nor is it limited to the eight major sites. Much more is available, ranging from 'Sir Harry Lauder's Music Hall Costumes, and curly walking sticks' to the Museum of Scottish Leadmining, 'one of our charming museums for a taste of life in days gone by'. Despite such lapses into cliché, this varied past is presented to the reader with commendable restraint. And the whole has clearly cost a lot of time, effort and money to bring to the state when, quite apart from local functions, it can be offered for visitor use so confidently. Interestingly, a similar note of modest pride was struck by Strathclyde Regional Council in its 1988 Glasgow Garden Festival leaflet. It highlighted its Regional Archive of historical records on 'five and a half miles of shelves'.

Indeed, much of the tourist ephemera available in Scotland is relatively restrained in its language, characteristically informational rather than aggressively promotional. The titles of two leaflets, *Architectural Heritage of Renfrew District* and *Eday Heritage Walk*, exemplify the point, and their prose substantiates it. The awful thought is that this compliment would be taken as a major criticism among so-called professional circles preying around the periphery of heritage tourism.

Of course, a general matter lies behind those Scottish excursions. Many organisations are increasingly looking to use their pasts, mainly out of economic desirability, sometimes necessity, within a political climate which has encouraged and even demanded that the past should pay its way. English Heritage, for example, has a statutory obligation to capitalise on the country's heritage resource in its care by making more, and more revenue-earning, use of it. Naturally, it looks to more customers through the turnstiles to produce figures appropriate for waving in front of its political paymasters, and hence all the 'events' at Properties in Care. There were dozens of them in 1990.

Even the more sober Royal Commission on the Historical Monuments of England has been told 'that we cannot expect the future funding of the National Monuments Record to come from national government sources alone' (though no reason is given for this presumably doctrinaire subjection of the curation of England's cultural memory bank to a level of public funding less than is implicitly acknowledged to be necessary). The Royal Commission is therefore assessing both 'the revenue likely to accrue from marketing information' and the organisational changes necessary 'in order to attract and manage revenue'. This may not appear to be directly connected with tourism, and indeed it is not in England, yet. But the similar Royal Commission in Scotland has already drawn heavily on its National Monuments Record in producing an excellent series of tourist-oriented books called *Exploring Scotland's Heritage*. Scholarship and market needs are meticulously and successfully melded in them. This seems a good thing in itself; given all the printed tourist pap available, it is particularly refreshing.

Nevertheless, England's two major official heritage bodies, carrying out public duties which used to be thought of as a matter of national pride, now have to use that of which they are the custodians, the one counting bums on seats as a measure of 'success', the other flogging data in substantial part, it might be observed, generated by the constituency which is envisaged as its 'market'. There is only a difference of degree here, not principle, in comparisons with local fund-raising efforts such as the village pantomime and the church bring-and-buy sale.

Local government is much involved in using the past too. Often it will want to promote any historic interest and sites in its area, not just to encourage more visitors and income but also to project a more favourable impression of the place; 'image repositioning' to use the jargon. Cities, notably Bradford and Glasgow, and towns such as Tunbridge Wells have used their pasts in both ways, and rural councils too have not been slow in seeking to image an identity around a core of historicity. Leeds provides a good example of an urban attempt at re-imaging; its Leisure Services' *Days Out* leaflet illustrates aspects of the past being used to tackle a perceived problem. The attempt both denies a past with which it is stuck and uses selective pastness to help reshape a new projection, partly for self-pride but very much with an eye to visitors and a place on the cognitive map of potential tourists.

'Images of Leeds', it begins, apparently boldly grasping the nettle, 'Victorian architecture' (ah yes, so we were right; but what's this?), 'tropical butterflies, rare breeds of cattle, exotic birds, cool woodland, kingfishers and sparrow-hawks and beautiful gardens'. Well, good try, one might respond, but that is not what appears to pass before the eye as the trans-Pennine train crawls through the Leeds conurbation. But all becomes clear: the problem is not Leeds itself but our preconceptions of it. 'Forget about dark, satanic mills, cloth caps, and clogs', we are exhorted, for Leeds is a green and cultured place. And the new past appropriate to such a scenario consists of a quite stunning assemblage, according to the blurb. Middleton Park is 'a wonderful area of ancient woodland and tracks' 'steeped in early industrial history', with access from Middleton Steam Railway, 'the oldest commercial railway in the world'. In Kirkstall Valley Park, 'The Museum Trail links forty historic sites . . .' including 'probably the finest Cistercian ruin in the country' and the Abbey gatehouse in which 'is a series of full size Victorian streets'. Temple Newsam is 'a 1000 acre estate with Tudor-Jacobean mansion' (containing 'one of the most important country house museums of decorative arts in England') and Home Farm where 'Piglets, turkeys and kittens run loose in the farmyard', 'Most of the cattle, pigs, sheep, goats, and poultry are Rare Breeds' and 'The old farm buildings house collections of farm implements and machinery and exhibits on farm life in yester-year'. And Lotherton, 'an Edwardian country estate set in rolling countryside' has a Hall, 'Former home of the Gascoigne family' but now home to 'works of art from many different periods' including 'a splendid collection of Chinese ceramics'.

Gone indeed are clogs, caps and satanic mills: only one mill is allowed to exist in this post-modernist pastoral landscape of authentic components and rearranged integrity. Thoroughly under heritage control, tamed today as an industrial museum, Armley Mills was once the world's largest woollen mill; but now it 'reverberates to the sound of working machinery' only during Working Weekends. Surely a certain pathos lurks here?

And what of the City itself, for surely the view from the train is not entirely apparition? Well, it is worth all of 'a couple of hours' of your time and contains three elements: 'The superb Victorian Arcades', 'the Georgian squares and streets' of the West End which are, however, 'just as fine'; and 'tucked away amongst the shopping streets . . . the pubs and yards laid out in the 14th century'.

All credit to Leeds for putting so much enlightened self-interest into the care and presentation of its selected past, for the use of citizen as well as visitor; and to the thinkers and writers of its Leisure Services for such a superb repackaging job. Theirs is a classic example of not just successful verbal gentrification and bucolicisation of a most unlikely subject but also a triumphant exercise in de-urbanisation. Paradoxically, as ever, in creating a 'Leeds' attractive to visitors in significant part by using their historic assets, they have actually denied Leeds its history as an important city. Nevertheless, next time my train crawls through those apparently small islands of lugubrious and soggy semi-dereliction between prairies of parkland and forests of sylvan delights, I shall look with renewed interest at the visually drear and bulky evidence of Leeds's particular historic importance, that is as an urban manufacturing centre (Pl. 36).

Leeds must stand as metaphor for urban council use of pasts, a huge subject. Think of the analogous, but different, images, conjured up by Nottingham's welcome to the 'City of Lace and Legend'. For comparison, try Langbaurgh's 'Heritage Route', a brave attempt to provide identity as well as attraction in a non-area. Well, do you know where Langbaurgh is? Perhaps the answer, 'In the eastern part of Cleveland', does not help much, that county being both a modern creation and still probably unlocated in most people's cognitive geography. 'Across the River Tees, immediately south of Middlesbrough', might help in locational terms but probably does not immediately promote irresistible urges to visit. Clearly the Borough Council has problems: how does it get on to the map?

One answer is to grasp every bit of available pastness, fling them into 'A Journey Through Time' and stir vigorously in a leaflet financially assisted by the Regional Tourist Board. Ingredients include Romans, Vikings, Norse names, Normans, a priory, civil war skirmishes, cannon fire heard in 1779 when 'Paul Jones the American buccaneer attacked Skinningrove', architectural heritage, Sir William Turner's Hospital, Ormesby Hall, maritime heritage, 'Zetland', the world's oldest surviving lifeboat, iron ore as the key to Victorian prosperity, industrial heritage, churches, Tocketts Water Mill, Saltburn as a 'quiet, period resort' with 'the oldest remaining water-balance cliff railway in Britain', Rushpool Hall 'with its links with Lawrence of Arabia', and Captain James Cook RN whose 'many voyages of discovery are part of our National Heritage'. The leaflet does not mention that the last is located elsewhere, according to a rival geography, in 'Captain Cook Country', not to be confused with 'Catherine Cookson Country' further up the Northumbrian coast (in Tourist Board Terms, though actually in the County of Tyne and Wear which has as much historical validity as Cleveland, above p. 49). Where everything is heritagised, how can we tell where we are?

We might even be in the south of England, for the landmarks of 'White Horse and Cotswold Country' are remarkably similar in general. At least Leeds and Langbaurgh did not have to invent a place: Leeds exists, even if the right sort of history for it in the late twentieth century did not, and so does Langbaurgh albeit less convincingly. 'White Horse and Cotswold Country', in contrast, is fabrication, especially in tandem. Are they one or two 'Countries'? – the implication is that they are/it is one. Each component has historic roots. The 'White Horse' is the late prehistoric chalk-cut figure at Uffington on the north face of the Berkshire Downs, now in Oxfordshire. Below it, imprecisely defined, is the Vale of the White Horse, a name sanctified by literary usage as much as anything. Alfred Williams, for example, wrote about the *Villages of the White Horse* (1913). The Cotswold Hills (or just 'the Cotswolds') is the traditional name, of Anglo-Saxon origin, of the limestone (not chalk: cf. above p. 36) uplands between Bath and north-east Gloucestershire.

The leaflet in effect enticing us to WH & C Country emanated from the Thamesdown and District Tourist Association, introducing another invented name. 'Thamesdown', an elision of River Thames and the Marlborough Downs, came into existence in 1972 as a label for a newly-defined district council area centred on Swindon: you can see the problem. The 'Country' of the leaflet stretches from the Bristol Channel in the west across to Newbury in Berkshire, and from Burford in Oxfordshire to the north as far as Trowbridge in Wiltshire. In other words, it has no being at all, and certainly no historical basis, except as an organisational convenience in touristic terms. As might be expected, this bogusness is reflected in the catholic, unrelated string of attractions gracing the landscape of a non-Country.

The use of pastness in tourism is nevertheless a serious business, as figures quoted elsewhere in this book indicate (above p. 6 and p. 62). Equally, tourism has a major impact on those very places people wish to tour to, *in extremis* leading to the destinations actually being closed or managed with various forms of 'people rationing' (above p. 81). Has the present generation the right to deny access to its contemporaries, real people now, in the long-term interests of some impersonal structure? – many of those contemporaries would deny that right, and frequently do when frustrated at a closed or only partially accessible site. Equally, given the conservation ethic, do we not as the contemporary stewards of a cultural inheritance have a duty to look after it in order to pass it on to posterity? Many people accept that principle too, and the practical constraints which it places on their personal freedom. By and large, the tourist industry has still to learn that lesson and absorb its implications. Without doing so, it will be just another exploiter of heritage, and one would hope it would not wish to be, or be seen to be, that alone.

Exploiting the past 11

Some exploitation of the past is very obvious. Benson and Hedges' promotion of their cigarettes with large poster photographs of the Egyptian pyramids is a case in point. There is not of course any historical association between cigarettes and pyramids of any period, type or place. B & H have invented the link, and with their product in particular. The fact that the resultant image is the first to come to mind in starting this chapter will doubtless be taken as indicating the success of, indeed the justification for, their creative exploitation of a powerful part of the past. Presumably they are seeking to ride to their own ends the positive images – of permanence, antiquity, regality, exoticism, not to mention rectangularity? – of their new-found pyramidical partners. In so doing, however, they have not only colonised to their own supposed advantage one of the very few global images – Stonehenge is another – of pastness (Pl. 37); they have also hijacked a myriad individual pasts genuinely associated with the Egyptian pyramids. This is not just exploitation; it is abuse. 'Think of pyramids and think of B & H' is one thing; 'think of B & H and think of pyramids' is quite another. 'How dare they?' could well be an outraged reaction; 'they have taken over by association part of my past'. In terms of image, at least, a corporation has taken unto itself part of the common heritage.

To say as much is, of course, to make a value judgement; and there is indeed a fine line here, between 'exploitation' and 'abuse', just as there was in Chapter 9 between 'use' and 'exploitation'. The difficulty is identifying where or when 'use' becomes 'exploitation', mainly because the difference is more a matter of motivation and intent – self-interest in a word – rather than physically distinct manifestations or destructive actions. Nevertheless, the range of exploitation of the past is enormous, and much of it fairly common, so a few examples must suffice.

Let us begin at the 'soft' end of the range with 're-creation', a common enough activity in the heritage field. Take, for example, Butser Ancient

Farm in Hampshire, not in image or intent an obvious case of exploitation of the past (Pl. 38). The project is primarily and fundamentally about research, its premises an open-air laboratory for experiment in late pre-historic agriculture. Over nearly twenty years it has accumulated a vast amount of data which, not without controversy, has contributed significantly to late twentieth-century understanding of farming in Britain in the last centuries BC. At an early stage, back in the 1970s, popular interest in seeing what was going on made it necessary to provide a demonstration area, initially to protect the experimental area from visitors but soon for its own sake as an educational and revenue-earning facility. Over some fifteen years, the research project was basically kept going by the income from the latter. Exploitation? – no, for income was entirely, and literally, ploughed back into experiment and meanwhile a great deal was provided over the years to visitors and others.

Many school children, for instance, were introduced to concepts such as 'Iron Age', the practicalities of pre-modern farming, and methodologies of using evidence. Despite similarities in appearance, academically and in motive the whole was of a different order from the transitory BBC 'Iron Age Village' of 1978 (above p. 16). In a sense, in completely eschewing the human element as a part of the experimental research, Butser is dull, for science demands the minimalisation of the human factor; but meanwhile it has contributed significantly to late twentieth-century understanding of late prehistory, using the past to know the past. Nevertheless, an honest penny was turned from time to time by, for example, open days at which people could play at firing 'ancient pots', and by 'Celtic feasts' in the great round house. Now, its lease terminated, the whole project has moved to continue its research on new land with the intention that henceforth it can flourish by its own entrepreneurial devices, independently of the fitful supply of research grants and charity. The new site has therefore been planned *ab initio* not just to take visitors but to attract them, and in large numbers too. Income from this source, in what is now envisaged as a marketing operation, will make or break the project as a provider of educational services and conductor of basic research. The situation is already one all too familiar at numerous similar enterprises, essentially academic and altruistic but of necessity forced increasingly to become more commercial – and therefore more exploitive? It is indeed a nice dilemma: to take, even to make, what cash is swilling around out there beyond the bounds of history at the risk of deflection from the real purpose and of tarnishing the academic image? Or to remain pure and go under?

In these days of curtailed research grants and entrepreneurial acceptability, even the past as a research field seems able only to survive by trading in some of its purity, by cashing in on aspects of its public appeal. Perhaps it is naive *not* to do that. After all, many of the major expeditions, excavations and even whole museums have been funded in the past by benefactors, patrons and Trusts. What is the difference if we now take money off a willing public as well? To do so is a quantitative, not an ethical change, provided basic scientific objectives and academic integrity are always to the fore. That qualification is, however, the rub, and its avoidance is the first easy step to take in exploitation.

The Demonstration Area at the first Butser was a creation, though each of its physical components was based on good evidence. (It was all destroyed by the end of September 1990, so has itself now become part of history and the area it occupied a new, precisely dated archaeological site – of a 1970/80s version of an archaeological site some 2,200 years earlier!) Nevertheless, there was nothing on the site beforehand to reconstruct and no single site elsewhere of which it is an attempted reconstruction. It was an authentic fantasy.

Less fantastic, in that there was more to start from, but likewise attempted re-creations are serious efforts to reconstruct specifics. The short lengths of 1970s Hadrian's Wall at Vindolanda ('We find the things Pompeii can't'), one mile south of the real thing, is a good example. It was built 'to show the size and strength of the original frontier' and, like the Butser House, as a crowd-puller. It has been criticised both as a structure and for being built where it is, i.e. not only not on or beside the prototype but as an addition to an authentic Roman fort of which the essence is precisely that it originated not only before the Wall itself but before a mural frontier had been conceptualised. Vindolanda now, being therefore visually what it could never have been then, marks a step towards the modern creation of an archaeological zoo or, as they are called in the commercial leisure world, 'theme parks' (below p. 133).

Not that there is anything new under the sun; a headline (*DT*, 17 December) announced the discovery of 'The world's oldest theme park for tourists'. It was 'the spectacular Persian Portico in Sparta', 'a prominent ancient ruin at the foot of Sparta's acropolis' currently being excavated. Believed to be a second-century AD Roman rebuilding of a fifth-century BC war memorial, such an interpretation, remarks the article's academic author, 'fits nicely with what else we know about Roman Sparta's heritage industry'.

Albeit entirely different in motivation, modern theme parks are conceptually similar to the Scandinavian-pioneered open air museum of regional historic buildings brought together centrally, conserved and displayed, each for its own sake but of course out of context. Inadvertently in a sense, the new context overall is entirely a creation, a new settlement of which the appearance conditions our appreciation of the authentic individual buildings. In that respect, they are exactly the same as a traditional indoor museum where the individual objects are displayed not only out of context but in a new fabricated one which affects our perception. Neolithic stone axes, for example, were never meant to be 'used' in rows as a satisfyingly-shaped mural seen through glass on a purple cloth backing.

Recognising this, consciously new 'towns', not of new buildings but of previously unassociated old ones reformatted into new spatial configurations, are now being carefully created at, for example, the Weald and Downland Museum, Sussex, Blists Hill, Ironbridge, and Beamish, County Durham. They emphasise the typical and workaday rather than the exotic and aesthetic. Meticulously researched but nevertheless collectively what never was in fact, they project a markedly functional, vernacular profile. Reflecting the contemporary emergence of interest in social history, they cock a snook at the more traditional 'top people's past' projected by cathedrals, castles and country houses. They symbolise the common man's past of labour, neighbour and netty (Pl. 39) as distinct from the national past of Blenheim and Tower of London. In contemporary terms, this is heritage 'Coronation Street', not Clark's 'Civilisation', the takeover by 'EastEnders' rather than 'The Triumph of the West', a development greeted with as much approval, incidentally, in the Labour Party's current environmental policy document as the disapproval in other circles for a recent exhibition in the Barbican in like vein about 'The Edwardians'. Politics are never very far from the past. It would be nice to think that these two sorts of modelled heritage form a whole but they seem to be consumed not as different facets of an homogenous past but as two separate and unrelated things – menus, as it were, at different take-aways.

It is a huge intellectual leap, but a short step, from historically-based re-creations to 'The Bygone Village'. The phrase is used generically, but there is actually one called that in East Anglia. It is of course a commercial venture first and foremost, very different in origin from Butser and such as the Weald and Downland Museum, Sussex, and different from but getting closer to some aspects of Blists Hill and Beamish. Its thirty-two components, however, are a dead giveaway, an eclectic *compote* of the authentic and the cliché. They include, in no particular order, a Souvenir Barn, a Railway Station, a Market Garden, a Village Hall, a Pets Paddock, a Smithy, an Owl Enclosure, a Village Green, Almshouses, a Chipmunk Picnic Garden and a Crazy Golf Course. Special attractions embrace 'One of the finest Showman's engines in the Country', 'The fabulous G4 Gavioli organ', 'the famous celebrity loco, No. 1928, previously used in the James

Bond film *Octopussy*', and 'A full size Swedish Railcar'. Who needs history when there's 'The Bygone Village'?

It is, however, not hard to take further steps along the road to the demeaned as well as deconstructed past. 'Poldark' in Cornwall, physically very similar in its components to 'Bygone' but with a hard core of a real tin-mine, is after all seeking to create a reality in a fictional place-name given common currency by a television serial (the cheat being that many presumably think that Poldark really existed and here it is). Historical fiction becomes present fantasy, both vaguely cotton-woolled in a sort of pastness. A minor variant on such exploitation comes by mixing indiscriminately fact and fiction, genuine and spurious, the historical and the fantastic, but all without using any authentic 'hard core' in the way that the tin-mine is shown at Poldark.

Thursford, also in Norfolk, exemplifies the formula: 'Old farm buildings, transformed into a mini-village with a touch of Charles Dickens' England ... a light snack under the fine timbers of our traditional Norfolk barn ... [nearby] a period-style ice-cream parlour ... take a nostalgic trip back to childhood – either on Thursford's narrow-gauge railway (where you can re-live all those wonderful sounds and smells of the steam age); or on our switchback roundabout with its Venetian gondolas ... Walk into a glittering Aladdin's Cave of majestic old road engines; and mechanical organs of magical variety all gleaming ...' Enough said: exploitation can be recognised for what it is when it appears.

Essentially the phenomenon exemplified there is of course selling a sort of past, verging towards selling *per se* by exploiting pastness. This whole area of activity is deeply embedded in commerce and business, and in the tourism and leisure industries in particular. Commercial theme parks, existing for profit by providing entertainment for a leisure-seeking public, are outstanding in their exploitation of pastness, either in part, as at Thorpe Park, or as their base. 'Camelot', an obvious and pretty tatty-looking eruption into the landscape as visible from the M6 motorway, is really not much more than an old-style fun fair dressed up in Arthurian clichés packaged with dreadful inevitability for 'the family day out'. Not far to the south is 'Frontierland' on the sea-front at Morecambe, a similar installation façaded loosely and with little regard for authenticity or integrity around a perception of the North American frontier in the nineteenth century (Pl. 40). In both cases, history as such clearly does not matter; it merely provides a convenience packaging to image a leisure product.

New is the idea of creating such a leisure centre on a green field site, as at Thorpe Park, Camelot and, with its marginal reference to history,

Alton Towers. All are conveniently close, like the 'big shed' distribution centres of consumer businesses, to access points on the motorway network. All seek, wholly or partly through a new pastness, an individuality; indeed each seeks, with a touching disregard for absolutes, to be more unique than the next. 'Frontierland's' ubiquitous wooden façadism, superficially carrying through its historical theme, is presumably intended as an aid to characterisation (and note how I carried away that image) and to give a bit of life to what would otherwise be just another of those sad and so often bedraggled fun fairs which litter English seaside holiday resorts.

Personally, I found 'Frontierland' pathetic and – my strongest take-away image – deeply offensive in its casual, inaccurate and ignorant portrayal of indigenous North American peoples. Perhaps the offence was unintentional, neither knowingly racist nor deliberately demeaning of what in popular perception are, after all, mere 'Indians'. Yet the whole is boorish, an unacceptable and insensitive treatment of complex, deeply historical cultures whose integrity Western Whites are only now coming to appreciate. Furthermore, just beneath the surface of 'Frontierland's' glib tableaux are profound and delicate issues of the present day, and not just in the USA.

Yet, by certain criteria, it is a success: 'The top attraction opening since 1985 is Frontierland in Morecambe with an estimated 1.2m visits' (in 1989, the latest year for which figures are currently available; *LN*, 6 December, quoting the English Tourist Board).

The leisure world has a horrible fascination. For one thing it is profoundly educational for the person who starts from the premises that history is worth studying for its own sake and that the present has a responsibility for the past based on informed stewardship. It was a world revealed by its own journalistically successful and (often more than it probably realised) informative 'professional' magazine *Leisure News*, a weekly which sadly itself became part of history as this chapter was being written. Heritage on the hoof indeed! Where now the window through which to espy that Wonderland landscape in which the Tower of London is a 'top venue' (in third spot of the national league table as a matter of fact, with 2.21 million visitors in 1989) and 'the Albert Dock in Liverpool beat the British Museum to second place with 5.1m visits' in the category of 'free admission attractions'? (first was Blackpool Pleasure Beach with an estimated 6.5 million visitors). This is real-time heritage where the bucks stop.

Virtually any issue of *Leisure News* illumined various aspects of exploiting pastness, and always in the same frenetically deadpan prose which reported it (and why should it do otherwise?) as any other commodity in a multi-million pound, but financially sensitive, enterprise ('a record 330m visits in 1989 generated £700 million...'). Other relevant items in the 6 December issue alone, for example, included a proposed 'Heart of Lancashire' leisure village, developing 'redundant farm buildings along-side the Leeds–Liverpool canal'; a proposed '... 40,000-seater stadium with tractable roof and floating pitch ... and a host of theme park, museum and conference facilities'; 'applications for funds for capital projects which would include development of the Beamish Museum and Kilhope Wheel lead mine'; and 'plans to build [a] holiday village at the Longleat Estate...'. Also included were news of the threat to a privately-owned tropical rainforest in Hampshire by the County Council's plan 'to restore the former glasshouses of Sir George Staunton, an eminent Victorian plant collector' and of 'A group of Kent railway enthusiasts ... looking to raise £60,000 to build a museum to house its collection of steam locomotives, carriages and rail artefacts'. A double page *Profile* of the retiring Chairman of the National Trust saw her 'leaving a battle raging between traditionalists and the newer breed of supporter', by implication relating to the innocently question-begging assumption contained in the laconic phrase 'now that heritage has gone commercial...'.

Among property for sale was, of course, a Georgian mansion 'ripe for hotel or country club conversion' (and the advert really did say that; guide price £2.5 million. Cf. Pl. 41 in which the Georgian hotel is ripe for conversion in the other direction); a 'substantial Estate with *potential for golf/hotel development...*' and, with notable honesty, a 'semi derelict Grade II Hall ...'; and 'a magnificently restored 19th century theatre ...'. Big Country Motioneering Ltd ('Thrills and Fantasies in motion') drew attention to the availability of 'veteran cars' along with its portable log flumes and Hari Kari system.

Appointments in this dynamic field were instanced in the public sector by an advertisement for the vacant Head of Cultural and Information Services at Wigan (with responsibilities for the Pier and the Turnpike Centre, naturally, and also for contributing 'to the development of tourism and the economic growth of the Authority'). The private sector, represented by 'Heritage Projects', wanted a marketing manager for 'The White Cliffs Experience' which, opening in 1991, 'will tell the frontline story of Dover in an innovative and educational way'. Needless to say, you had to be 'highly motivated'. But that alone was insufficient: in a classic example of a lyrical job-description, 'To succeed in this challenging role you must be an experienced marketeer, at ease with all aspects of the marketing mix. You must be a creative thinker, self-motivated and used to a hands-on approach.' Of course such verbiage is normal in its own world; it just reads flatulently in another world of normality. Does this saleman's job really need such talent? And is such talent really well-employed in flogging off a show-piece past?

Yet, in both the worlds of hype and normality, new threats to our heritage have emerged, according to *Leisure News*'s tongue-in-cheek tailpiece, so to speak. The effect of human breath and body temperature on Palaeolithic paintings has for long occasioned the closing of famous caves in France. Now, 'Scientists have concluded that the main Art gallery pollutant ... is the human fart. And ... another danger comes from the wet clothes of soggy tourists ...'.

The deduction is obvious, and of great cheer to the heritage business: far from these (quite serious) scientific findings leading to the collapse of touristic heritagism as we all stop visiting that huge, invaluable and irreplaceable part of our genuine heritage indoors, the past exploiters can look forward to a booming future. Clearly it should be encouraged, most of all by its main critic, the conservation lobby. Entrepreneurs must build more and more theme parks, 'historic' and otherwise, at *every* motorway interchange (building on the percipient comments of Martin Pawley, BBC 2, 30 December). Their whole operation can be done mechanically and under computer control, modelled on the distributive procedures of large service companies; no tourist need depart from tarmac or concrete, the countryside will be inviolate and traffic will declutter historic towns. The more people that go to the 'Big Sheds of History', the better; perhaps they should even be subsidised. In this way we can, at one and the same time, provide efficiently and cleanly for mass tourism, clearly quite happy with pastiche and surrogate, while saving our real past in museums and galleries empty of polluting people and full of pure air.

One of the saddest contemporary sinners in the exploitation stakes is perhaps the most surprising: the Ordnance Survey. One of its recent feats illustrates just how deeply pursuit of market-led commodification has affected both a product and what used to be a public service. Of great and deserved prestige as a cartographic agency over two centuries, the OS has throughout that time pursued an archaeological interest, doubtless minor in relation to its main purposes but of great significance in the development of an awareness of the past in Britain's landscape. Despite an understandable militarist philistinism towards such matters in its corporate psyche, a succession of individuals has persevered with the laudable objective of surveying, and making publicly available on the country's official maps, visible and invisible ('Site of') 'Antiquities', cartographically displayed in distinct letter-faces. These are archaeological structures such as hillforts and castles, the find-spots of particular but unassociated evidence such as hoards of prehistoric metalwork and Roman pottery, and the sites of events such as Civil War battlefields.

Behind this public face of its role in matters archaeological and historic, for the last seventy years the Survey has been supported by a line of distinguished academics, both as its Archaeology Officer and in advisory roles. They endeavoured to ensure that its material was not only correctly located but also interpretatively well-informed. As a result of this tradition of scholarship, the Survey developed the additional capacity to prepare and publish 'Period Maps', as in its popular and highly influential *Map of Roman Britain*, thematic maps, as in *Long Barrows of the Cotswolds*, and detailed maps of particular areas and monuments. York, for example, has recently been accorded two maps, respectively embracing *Roman and Anglian York* and *Viking and Medieval York*, both published as the result of considerable academic co-operation led by the Royal Commission on the Historical Monuments of England. This body became official academic adviser to the OS when, in the white heat of Civil Service rationalisation and quango-hunting which characterised the first Thatcher government, the Survey's archaeological functions were transferred, with severely curtailed resources of course, to it. In effect, the OS then became a user of the past instead of being a generator and public supplier of it. Now, as with its other data, it sells it, and some results of the change have quickly become apparent.

One of the Survey's best-ever archaeological maps (1964) was of a single monument, Hadrian's Wall, marvellously depicted in its frontier context in a wide swathe across northern England. On its publication, the map was recognised for what it was: a monument to the cartographer's art and high scholarship as much as to the Wall itself. And it played fair to the public by being thorough, honest and up-to-date. Archaeologically and historically an outstanding monument of the Roman Empire, the Wall's academic importance has been supplemented in recent times by its increasing role in tourism and as an amenity. Part of the Pennine Way passes along it; much of its central section on the Whin Sill crags is in a National Park, belongs to the National Trust and/or is in the Guardianship of English Heritage; the whole, with surrounding landscape, now has the status of World Heritage Site (Pl. 12). In other words, the Wall zone is regarded as important by many people. The Ordnance Survey, doubtless responding to this perception, and seeing in it the chance of profitable sales, recently published a third edition of its Hadrian's Wall map. It is a cheapjack insult to the Wall, its archaeology and landscape, and to those who value and use them. It demonstrates, as in some Jorvik imitations without the substance, exactly what can happen when scholarship and integrity are abandoned, consciously in this case, in a misconceived, downmarket quest in pursuit of commercial opportunism. It is not even an acceptable map in cartographic terms, never mind its mindless archaeology.

Past workings

What a fall from grace! And what a cheat to the public, the tourists, the walkers, the teachers and their pupils, and the archaeologists whose work, so often done with public money for the public, is ignored! All have a right to expect something much better than this *apologia* for things past, an *apologia* which says more about the spirit of the times and its erosion of the concept of public service by commodification than it does about the glory that was Rome.

23 A rare case of a Scheduled Ancient Monument also being a 'honeypot' heritage site: the much-repaired 'old' (but certainly not prehistoric) Tarr Steps over the River Barle at a visitor mecca on Exmoor, Somerset.

24 The grandiloquent past voices imperial confidence and Edwardian panache in the form of the Williamson Memorial, Lancaster, a Grade I Listed Building recently renovated at considerable expense as the focus of its beautifully-kept municipal park, green and tidy even in the August of a long, hot summer. It has also acquired a contemporary, originally unconceived function as striking eye-catcher from the nearby M6 motorway.

5 Archaeological survival as separate and isolated monuments in a working agricultural landscape: Fortingall stone settings, Loch Tay, Perth and Kinross.

6 Eroding the past: a combination of quarrying and cattle hoof-prints expose and destroy the fragile interleaving of wind-blown sand and archaeological layers which make up the mound of Saevar Howe, near Birsay, Orkney Mainland.

27 The site of long-term archaeological excavations on a National Trust property in a Country Park, Crickley Hill hillfort, Gloucestershire, displays across part of its interior low modern posts marking the positions of timber uprights which framed late prehistoric rectangular and circular buildings. Beyond is an excavated entrance and inner rampart, with viewing platform and information boards.

Concrete tries to imitate nature as it is cleverly striated in a modern man-made cliff formed by the Scottish Ancient Monuments Inspectorate. It is designed to protect in sympathetic manner from further marine erosion the multi-period settlement in the care of the state on the Brough of Birsay just off the north-west coast of Orkney Mainland.

The cabin'd and confin'd past as represented by The Whispering Knights, Rollright, Oxfordshire, outliers of the Rollright stone circle. This early example of an official Ancient Monument shows it being preserved by a usually dominant and fiercesome fence which separates it from its context as well as protecting it from the plough; but note the erosion caused by visitors' feet around the enclave.

143

30 The recently-improved, sunken entrance to Stonehenge, noon, 15 August

31 Scholars on the 1989 Hadrian's Wall Pilgrimage earnestly debate mural minutiae *in situ*, led by the la Chief Inspector of Ancient Monuments for England and the about-to-become First Chief Inspector of Ancient Monuments, Historic Buildings and Monuments, Scotland.

32 Who owns Stonehenge? I days of yore – 1968 is the da of this photograph – people used to be able to walk amo the stones and perhaps be lucky enough to hear a schoolteacher explaining the monument to pupils. But the experience was at the cost o an unaesthetic concrete 'floc thinly covered with gravel to take the wear and tear of fee and of damage to the stones from grit in the soles of footwear worn by people climbing on the stones. Now the interior is back to pleasi grass but visitors cannot ent during normal opening hour or at all on certain days of t year.

3 The Director of the York Archaeological Trust explains to undergraduates studying 'Heritage, Management and Society' as a final year special subject at the University of Newcastle upon Tyne the concept of the Archaeological Resource Centre opened in 1990 in a redundant church.

4 Heritage consumption exemplified by the lure of railwayana: working replica of Locomotion No. 1, star attraction of the Stockton-on-Tees display at the National Garden Festival, Gateshead, being filmed for TV. The participants may look like nostalgia enthusiasts but were actually the anxious film crew watching, not history in motion, but their camera between the rails as the replica was about to pass over it.

35 'Old England XI', essentially 1950s vintage, reconstituted to mark what at the time (July) was thought would be the last Caller's International Cricket Festival, Jesmond, Newcastle upon Tyne (subsequently announced as continuing under new sponsorship in 1991 by Heritage Homes, cf. Pl. 45). The two umpires flank the back row, with the sponsor second from left. Names thereafter, doubtless meaningless to many but the stuff of legend and nostalgia, great deeds and summer memories to others, are (from memory, for these are heroes of the author's youth) Colin Cowdrey, Tony Lock, Ted Dexter, Fred Trueman, Brian Statham; (front row) Godfrey Evans, Reg Simpson, Tom Graveney, Peter May, Dennis Compton and Trevor Bailey.

36 Urban heritage, commercial history and local authority tourist label: plaque on building, Little Germany, Bradford, West Yorkshire (March).

37 Colonisation of the past gives one answer to 'Who owns Stonehenge?' Throwaway cardboard cups provide the opportunistic medium for corporate promotion on the back of a well-known World Heritage Site which was given to the British nation in 1918.

8 An archaeologically justifiable past for research and public participation is illustrated in bulk and texture at the Demonstration Area of the Butser Ancient Farm, near Petersfield, Hampshire. This was a 1980s life-size realisation based on careful interpretation of scientific evidence of what an 'Iron Age farm' might have looked like c. 300 BC in southern England. It was demolished in September.

9 Industrial heritage, preserved and working for education and tourism: looms in operation, Quarry Bank Mill, Styal, Cheshire (June).

40 A careless past, cobbled together in a theme park purely as commercial entertainment: the Haunted Silver Mine, Frontierland, Morecambe, Lancashire (August).

41 Developing the past and exploiting the word 'heritage', exemplified by the proprietorial board of Heritage Properties on the Georgian façade to an older building, until 1990 the Hare and Hounds public house, Watlington, Oxfordshire. According to local rumour, John Hampden stayed there on the night before the battle of Chalgrove Field where he was fatally wounded in 1643. It flanks the market place dominated by the much-restored and rare Restoration (1665) Town (formerly Market) Hall (May).

Past projections

Then now, present and future **12**

Sir Isaiah Berlin was quoted as saying 'To dictate to the future is always a form of despotism. The important thing is Now.' (O, 14 October). Here it seems appropriate to ponder some of the generalities arising from the presence of the past in the present and, at the risk of despotism, to air some thoughts about possible pasts in the future. On the latter, it is perhaps worth stressing immediately that, certainly in archaeological terms and in historical ones too, some aspects of the future past are already circumscribed not just by what we have already allowed to be destroyed but also by what we have consciously decided to preserve. Both what has gone, and what will be there as a result of actions already taken, will shape, in intellectual as well as physical terms, parts of posterity's thoughts about its heritage.

For 'Now', however, there can be no sharp, pithy conclusion. It is already history that *The Death of the Past* was published in 1969, and that *The End of History* was so fashionably discussed in the late 1980s. Yet somehow the past seems to go on; not just pressing closer and closer on our presents but forever creating itself before our eyes and even anticipating its own arrival. In BBC TV's 'House of Cards' (November–December 1990), for example, viewers witnessed a fictional political future mimic current affairs as they themselves were very consciously turned into history. Indeed, in the fall of Mrs Thatcher, a particular branding of history was being *anticipated* before the event: Britain's first woman Prime Minister was already being written down as 'great', her place in history 'secure', some time in advance of her actual resignation.

With artefact rather than a person, as the vagaries of the leisure industry have waxed and waned, so there are now in the repertoire of England's landscape variety the archaeological sites of 1980s deserted theme parks: the remnants of one, for example, lurk in the undergrowth right beside the A30 in west Cornwall. It also came as something of a visual jolt, followed by a mental readjustment, to realise that a regular pattern of banks and platforms picked out in classically archaeological conditions by low winter sun in a grassy open space were not those of a deserted medieval village but part of a post-World War II New Town abandoned in 1989 (Pl. 42).

Even more immediately, at the moment that the Berlin Wall went down and we saw on television the first film of the physical consequences for it, I as an archaeologist was aware that we were witnessing the creation of an 'ancient monument', the making of a chunk of significant archaeology for which the immediate priority was not destruction but preservation. 'Instant archaeology' was happening before our eyes as a great military structure, immensely symbolic as well as deadly functional, became totally redundant in a matter of minutes, or so it seemed. Yet simultaneously it took on a new role as the major monument to a remarkable phase of European history abruptly ended, a physical structure paradoxically speaking about and to the future in terms of hope and, potentially, tourism.

The fate of the Berlin Wall, characteristically of the heritage field, aroused bitter controversy, for it was much hated, became a much-needed source of immediate cash, and yet was clearly of historical significance. Was a similiar debate held on Hadrian's Wall in 366, or in Royalist cities of England after their Roman and medieval walls had fallen to Cromwellian artillery? However that may be, reflect on how we value the remains of such walls now, on what they 'mean' as image-formers, as educational and tourist resources, as amenities and economic assets (Pl. 43). What would London or Bristol give now to have their walls back?

Of course by now the Berlin Wall has been much destroyed, prey to understandable obliteration and newly-expressed entrepreneurialism in the souvenir trade. It had to be an American who tried to have large chunks of it shipped across the Atlantic to break up into small bits for sale; it was along the Wall itself that early mornings saw Western capitalism in action as locals went to work with spray cans before chipping off their wares for the day. Painted bits of Wall, naturally, commanded higher prices than undistinguished fragments of what could, after all, have been any old bits of concrete (Pl. 44). There ought to be a 'lesson of history' in all this somewhere, perhaps even a 'moral of archaeology'. Anyway, it made a good piece of TV reportage in Channel 4's 'Down to Earth', not so much on the lines of 'the past in the present' which the series valiantly tried to project ('Archaeology is a £20 million business') as in vibes of 'the present becoming the past for the future'. That a stretch of the Berlin Wall is now to be rebuilt as a heritage and tourist attraction was entirely predictable, but it does not alter the fact that the future will have to be satisfied with a surrogate for the real thing.

Surely here is one of the identifiable traits of this curious late-twentieth-century phenomenon that the past has become. It is very much a phenomenon in the present about the present, but it also, sometimes consciously, is part of an incipient dialogue with the future (Pl. 45). Not that the thought is either new or agreed. Mark Twain wrote in 1877 that 'there was but one solitary thing about the past worth remembering and that was the fact that it is past – can't be restored'; and in a sense he was correct, philosophically and physically as in the case of the Berlin Wall. Yet Proust in *Remembrance of Things Past* allowed with somewhat grudging double negative that 'The past not merely is not fugitive, it remains present'. That it is artefact as well as present was, for example, the point made by Auden (*The Dyer's Hand*, 1962): 'Man is a history-making creature who can neither repeat his past nor leave it behind', as Berliners have just discovered. And it was Frederick Douglas who anticipated one of the thrusts of this essay in writing 'We have to do with the past only as we can make it useful to the present and the future' (*Life and Writings*, 1950, ed. P. S. Foner). This idea of 'a usable past' has most recently been explored in a book with that title by the American cultural historian William Bouwsma – which takes us back to Nietzsche's 'On the Uses and Disadvantages of History for Life' and the temptation to engage in one of the great philosophical debates of historiography.

Resisting that here, in what is meant to be more demonstration at a moment in time than exposition of the general, presumably these pages nevertheless exude some sympathy with Bouwsma's statement that 'History, much like water and electricity, is a public utility.' Of course, albeit incidentally, it suits my purpose here delightfully that that quotation, from the introduction to a book published in 1990, has already been overtaken *by* history. In the olde countrie of Britain, water and electricity are no longer public utilities but provided by share-based commercial companies. On the central matter, Bouwsma states his view unambiguously: '... history is not the private preserve of professional historians ... [who] are properly the servants of a public that needs historical perspective to understand itself and its values ... Historians have an obligation to meet public needs of this kind.' Substitute 'archaeologists' for 'historians' and the same is true.

By coincidence, the preface of another 1990 book asking the question 'Who owns Stonehenge?' remarked that, a decade ago, 'Intellectually, it belonged to the archaeologists, as the experts in these matters. The story is more complicated now ...', precisely because both a more extrovert professionalism and the pressure of external views have fragmented the assumption of the academic tradition that history/archaeology, and especially the sites of the latter, were the private preserve of the scholars in those fields. Just as education is far too important to be left to educationalists and teachers, the past is too important, especially in its multi-functionalism, to be left to the past practitioners. What we have been seeing in the 1980s, and see continuing into the 1990s, are the consequences of that, the breaking of an intellectual monopoly and the democratisation of an intangible at one level, of something very visual and sometimes tangible at another. The optimist would see good in this, a greater interest in history proper, a welcome popularity for the conservation and accessibility of the artefactual past; and he or she could well be justified. What is undeniable, however, is that uses of the past to meet that interest and popularity have fired the opportunists. The results include a powerful and doctrinaire political lobby, an influential commercially-driven point of view, a demeaning service industry, shallow, tawdry images of pastness, commodification and exploitation and, perhaps worst of all, a downmarket denial of proper access to its legitimate pasts to society whose very curiosity triggered the opportunity in the first place.

Not least because of the contemporary uses of the past, and its consequent debasement in many respects, it seems worthwhile reiterating that history still has a perfectly legitimate, and indeed fundamentally important, 'life' as a phenomenon well worth study for its own sake. Nor can the intellectual, educational benefits that its study provides be ignored. Furthermore, precisely because of its non-research uses, the sense of perspective history affords in time, and the rigorousness of its study at any one moment of time, are highly desirable parts of the late-twentieth-century social tool-kit. Physical survivals of the past are, selectively but for a variety of reasons, also well worth looking after, and the present rate and scale of their indiscriminate destruction is, in some categories, unacceptable on various grounds – for one thing it is foolish. The past is neither irrelevant nor a luxury nor meet merely for a 'backward-looking curiosity'. Rather is it significant and of concern to us in raising contemporary and future issues, not least about ourselves. Our attitudes to it, and its influence on us, seem to be inconsistent, heavy with ambivalence, and probably more important than we have yet realised. Nowadays, *more* pasts are more available in more forms to more people than at any time *in* the past; and they absorb more resources than ever before. Whether we have yet recognised that development, let alone faced its implications, is doubtful. Perhaps the scenario sketched here is a function of the post-industrial condition; possibly not recognising that to be so is part of the same state of mind.

In his influential state of the art book (1987), Hewison controversially pinpointed *The Heritage Industry* as symptomatic of a nation in decline. To talk of Britain in such terms was, of course, politically unacceptable at that moment: the Prime Minister and her government, vigorously still blowing on the Falklands embers, were bent on persuading the populace that 'Great' had been reinserted before Britain, a myth in which they apparently believed until her totally unexpected last day of office. There was also much talk of another phenomenon more apparent than real, 'the economic miracle'. Again that hardly provided an appropriate context in which to be publishing near-seditious literature about 'decline'. Furthermore, the heritage industry itself, having been unexpectedly given a group identity, reacted adversely to the idea that it was symptomatic of anything other than socially acceptable entrepreneurial flair in an increasingly sophisticated, affluent and leisure-seeking society. At least, that was the line from the commercial sector. The Establishment of public museums and galleries, of scholars and real professionals, simply objected to any suggestion that their activities had anything to do with an 'industry' (yet within four years early publicity was announcing a 1991 national conference on 'The Use of Drama in the Museums Industry'). As debate continued, so did the word 'heritage' come to be demeaned, leading to further disassociation between its meaning as an increasingly commercialised commodity and some components of the world it was meant to represent.

Hewison actually gave his titular phrase a fairly narrow sense. Primarily he meant the mainly commercialised 'industry' which had sprung up largely during the 1980s, manifesting itself across the landscape in hundreds of new or refurbished places ranging from proper museums through various forms of 'Heritage Centre' (his particular *bête noire*) to casually a-historical 'historical' theme parks. He had a point: like others, he was much taken by the oft-quoted statistic that, on average, one new museum opened every fortnight during the 1980s. Some of them would be encompassed in other numerical reflections of the trend: almost 40 per cent of all English 'attractions' have opened since 1980 and 600 'attractions' have opened since 1985 (*LN*, 6 December). Visits to historic properties between 1982 and 1989 increased by 30 per cent suggesting, incidentally, that they 'have not been adversely affected by the development of many new attractions during this period. Theme parks, for example, appeal to a different market and attract relatively few foreign tourists.' At least 1,793 historic buildings were open to the public in 1990, in England alone, to receive those non-theming foreigners.

Respecting Hewison's meaning, and declining to use it in a wider sense attempted by some others, preference is given here to the more appropriate phrase 'heritage business' to embrace the whole field of current activity relating to the past. Such a 'business' very definitely includes scholarship, proper academic museums, activities such as teaching archaeology, professional interpretation (of sites, landscapes), and conservation in all its senses, as well as the Hewisonian 'heritage industry'.

Past projections

A palpable change overcame the last during later 1990. Of course, the hype continued, and visitors continued to flock through its turnstiles; but the future of this sort of past began to look very different in the sensitive pages of its own *Leisure News*. Accurately doing its job of reporting trends and what was to be in the industry, its contents and editorial tone changed from upbeat and unquestioning confidence as the early indicators of economic recession spoke of new projects delayed, postponed and aborted and of the first closures, even bankruptcies and receiverships, on the existing scene. Scattered round the soft edges of the economy, dependent on the options in personal life-style being exercised in its favour, the economically marginal world of leisure development, of historic country house conversion and heritage day-out creation, began to send out early signals of recession, at least to itself, before the effects became apparent in more solidly-based activities. Heritage was quite suddenly no longer an easy passport to profitable commercial enterprise, nor will it be again in the immediate future. The same economic downturn also affects, as always, both the public sector and charitable parts of the heritage business where, despite the commitment to it for its own sake lacking in a theme park, for instance, financial realities are essentially the same. At a time of local authority cuts, for example, it is always the museum services, a non-statutory function, which are in the front line.

Economic constraints apart, some curious eddies and portents exist in other parts of the relationship between contemporary society and pastness. For example, how 'green' is the past? Indeed, is the present popularity of interest in various pasts stemming from the same basic urges that have given a public profile recently to environmental concern? Once more, answers are ambivalent. At an obvious level, 'greenness' has nothing to do with any past, and its publicity consciously avoids making any such link. The Friends of the Earth gift catalogue exudes a markedly different air from both that of the National Trust and, to take a commercial instance, the similar production of 'Past Times', 'a unique gift collection inspired by Britain's heritage'. At a more serious level, the essence of green thinking is forward-looking, as a philosophical and political necessity for one thing. The concern must be, and be seen to be, what our future environment is likely to be unless we change our ways, unless we move from exploitive, careless strategies to those based on concepts of renewable resources, finite resources and a more stable, even benign, relationship with Nature.

And yet, and yet ... While contemporary scholarship in history and archaeology may have no place in green thinking, part of its basic problem is of course precisely that current attitudes and organisations are themselves the products of the past. They are cultural phenomena. Thoughts on how to change them may well therefore be prompted by study of how they came to be. And resource management is now a concept fundamental to the care of archaeological heritage internationally and in many individual countries. In particular, the concept of physical survivals from the past being a finite resource has been common to professional heritage management since the 1970s, some time before the greening of the English language brought the phrase into popular use. That said, those looking after the past see a clear connection between what they are doing and environmental concern, to the extent that 'the historic environment' is conceived of and treated as part of the whole environment. Indeed an holistic approach here rejects what is regarded as a false dichotomy between natural and anthropogenic: the interrelationship is too complex for the whole to be thought of as other than a single biomass. 'Green' thinking has therefore supplemented and strongly influenced that of the past practitioners, who regret that what they have to offer, philosophically and practically, does not seem to be part of a bilateral awareness.

The National Trust is apt to part-explain the remarkable doubling of its membership from one to two million in the later 1980s as a reflection of the growth of popular conservation awareness – and, further, of peoples' wish to do something, to be involved, to make some sort of commitment even if it is only signing a subscription cheque once a year. If this perception is at all correct, then clearly a significant minority in society *do* see a connection between future and past and between natural and artefactual; and it may well be that a folk wisdom which detects the cultural dimension as part of long-term environmental relationships within the concept of communal stewardship is actually wiser than the pastless predictions of the gurus of greenery.

Conceptually and in practice archaeology has long been aware of the Man/Nature interface. Indeed, 'environmental archaeology' is a dynamic subset of the discipline. In conservation terms, the coincidence of cultural and environmental interests on the same sites has been a driving force for two decades. An eco-niche, for a particular plant community for example, is often precisely that because it is in land-use terms an undisturbed archaeological site. Many Sites of Special Scientific Interest are also places of archaeological interest, sometimes Scheduled Ancient Monuments; and *vice versa*. Some National Nature Reserves, designated for their 'natural' interest, not only accidentally contain archaeology but the latter can go a long way to explain the former. Nature, in Britain anyway, does not exist in a vacuum but nearly always in a cultural landscape: Fyfield Down on the Marlborough Downs is a classic example. Indeed, this recognition of mutual interests is now more a matter of professional symbiosis rather than seeing a link and it is curious that the green movement has excluded this well-documented development from its thought.

Similarly, by eschewing a backward-looking curiosity, 'greenery' does not appear to have taken aboard the potential of palaeo-environmental research. Results from this cannot be used to predict the future nor even to say what could happen; but by studying past man–environmental relationships patterns may well be perceived that can at least indicate parameters relevant to a consideration of a range of future possibilities. The hypothesis of 'global warming' and its causes are now well known and many people appreciate, without knowing the detailed science, that the 'prediction' is based on the establishment of a vast data-bank including past climatic records. The data are searched for patterns of various sorts and numerous future patterns of what might be are produced by extrapolation from the known and the perceived. However, in an historical sense there is nothing new in all this: prophets of the end of the world themselves form a characteristic pattern through time, especially in religious guise.

Furthermore, such 'ends' have actually happened, locally and regionally if not globally (but does the scale of catastrophe matter if you personally are one of the victims?). In this context, archaeology could be useful. We can reasonably interrogate our evidence to ask specific and general questions stemming from our present 'green' concerns. Archaeology has addressed with admirable scholarship the question of what sort of society it was that happened to be artefactually so well preserved on the Greek island of Santorini by the fall-out from the Theran volcano which destroyed it sometime between *c.* 1645 and 1500 BC. Can we not also ask how Aegean Bronze Age society reacted to such a cataclysmic event rather than confine ourselves to what happened before it? And are there in general any similarities, any patterns, in the behaviour of past societies face with such 'ends of the world as they knew it'? To have thought about this could at least give some perspective in time to the present 'green crisis', whether or not the thought helps us plan for the future or our successors to live it. To do as much would at least be to recognise a contemporary functional relevance of our systematic knowledge of the past rather than forever cocooning it, at least in its popular form, in 'the romance of archaeology/mystery of the past' school of presentation.

In Britain itself is a good example of how we could help ourselves by only connecting. The island is apparently threatened by rising sea-level and warmer climate. It has been through both before, several times. The evidence is there. We know in varying degrees of detail, accuracy and location what happened when much of eastern England was under water at different times in the past. We can interpret the evidence to different ends but surely one of them could be, indeed should be, to try to understand social reactions and environmental relationships that have already operated in such circumstances. Similarly, the British uplands would be drastically affected by an increase in the mean annual temperature of, say, 2°C and a drier climate. But why only best-guess what may happen should those circumstances return? During the third and second millennia BC, hundreds of thousands of people lived, bred, farmed, quarried and died up there, often, it seems, in organised communities working highly-managed landscapes. What were the secrets of their success? – we really ought to know and we certainly should not assume that the essentials of life four thousand years ago *in those circumstances* are irrelevant to us now as we contemplate the inheritance we might well bequeath to our successors (Pl. 46).

A related but different point, and one closer to the quasi-mystical core of some green belief, would be that we ought to rediscover such 'lost knowledge' anyway for its own sake as well as our self-interest. In living closer to Nature, so the argument runs, prehistoric people not only existed more harmoniously with their environment but were also privy to basic truths, about the universe, natural laws and so on, through a dimension of human sensitivity subsequently blunted and then lost. A lot of people actually believe this, one segment of that 'alternative' world ranging from 'hard', scientific greenery to the wilder shores of 'Gaia' now so voluminously represented on the 'New Age' shelves of the serious book-shops.

One prediction could well be that the numbers of such believers will grow as, in an increasingly uncertain but threatening future, individuals turn to the menu of available pasts in search of the course that meets their particular psychological and emotional needs now. The myth of the 'noble savage' is as good as any, its lack of scientific basis being for some an attraction rather than deterrent. At least it has a long and literary history, carrying through even into materialistic England today at the communal level in the romantic ideal of the non-existent rosy-cheeked and pipe-tamping rustic 'Urrring and Ahrrring' away over a frothy pint of unselfconsciously real ale by the thatch-beetled village green.

Another prediction can fairly safely be that such heritage 'chestnuts' as the sage old rustic will continue to be peddled and recycled. Indeed, maybe their range will narrow, their symbolism become more real, as the 'certainties' of scientific study of the past give way to more complexity and interpretive ambivalence while belief into any sort of future becomes more difficult. The present in the future could well tend to cling to the known whether it is scientifically known or not. The Isle of Man tries, for example, to tempt 1991 holidaymakers there by plastering London Underground stations with giant posters prominently featuring a bogus 'Viking' helmet with horns (Pl. 47). There is no scientific evidence for such horns, but we all 'know' that is what Vikings wore. At a more intellectual level, presumably the apparently insatiable appetite for still more about a fairly limited set of cultural pasts will continue to be met with books and articles, films and TV programmes on such topics as some Victorian novelists, the Bloomsbury set and the Impressionists while amazing new revelations will continue to be made about Piltdown Man, King Arthur (Pl. 48), Shakespeare, Mozart and Beethoven manuscripts, and who 'Mona Lisa' really was (this last information was actually provided, *post hoc scripto*, on 26 January 1991; but presumably not definitively).

Archaeological discoveries will also continue to be made; where they stem from excavation, versions of some of the discoveries will continue to be reported as news, but significant advances in knowledge will find if anything even more difficulty in commanding informed treatment in the public media. The potential of video, CADCAM and other high-tech media to present the past, and especially archaeology, on its own terms is enormous, and there will be significant developments here, especially at places of its own choosing on site, in museums and exhibitions, and in the classroom.

Indeed such media could well come to play a symbolic as well as practical role in the way society regards and uses its pasts. The 1990s may well see a reaction to tatty and spurious heritage, passive in its presentation and undemanding in its involvement. Rather will many want to know, not just what is known but how we know what we know, partly out of interest in the mechanics of how evidence is acquired and interpreted but also so that they can individually make up their own minds about its 'meaning'. There will be a tension here for, on the other hand, many will also be seeking some sort of refuge in the past and will prefer it pre-packaged and unquestioning. The heritage and tourist industries, targeting the older echelons of society seeking quality leisure-time, will doubtless play to this, not least mindful of the confident predictions of millions of pounds passing to the house-owning over-fifties as they inherit, with the death of their parents, the property values of the 1980s.

Such an approach, however, is hardly likely to satisfy many younger people, educated and working in a high-tech world where different 'answers' to a whole range of questions can be imaged by pressing a keyboard. The question will be not so much 'Was the past so different?' as 'Why should our images of a range of pasts be any different?' Using Stonehenge as metaphor once again, this raises a very practical point about what sort of interpretation(s) should be available about it, and the form in which they should be accessible, in the proposed new visitor centre there. It seems likely that the number and interpretations of images of the past will grow, increase and fragment. The idea of a homogenous past has already been overtaken by developments in British society and by events, not least in the very public discussions both triggered by the Salman Rushdie affair and about the schools history syllabus and its place in what is now very clearly a multi-ethnic society. Intellectually, a single agreed History of Britain is now conceptually and realistically impossible; it is probably undesirable too, again not so much because the past was not like that but, more pertinently, the past *is* not like that.

Another factor will come into play too. As we approach AD 2000 and the end of the millennium, the 1990s will witness an increasing and increasingly morbid *fin-de-siècle* search for roots in the past, for meaning in what has happened in the twentieth century. Given the soul-searching already exhibited every New Year and with the passing of each decade, the lead-in to 2000 will be long, maudlin and probably tediously morbid. Particularly will this be so with the dawning realisation that the twentieth century was *the* time to live in terms of social and personal well-being – if you were lucky enough to inhabit the Western world. But appreciation will simultaneously grow of the price, which is and will be that, in global terms, the twenty-first century can only go downhill. Will the twentieth century be tagged 'the irresponsible century'? – merely to ask the question is to anticipate a strong vein of questioning of the 'Where did we go wrong?' sort which will inevitably feature around the hinge of 2000 as the past is scrutinised by a society at least as much characterised by doubt and perhaps guilt as it will be by confidence and optimism.

Interacting with that strain on the past/present interface, nostalgia at a personal and local level will consequentially be rampant; and doubtless various commercial provisions will grow to service it. To everyone a family tree, to every place a potted history; each document personalised and unique, of course (but would you mind just filling in a few details like names in the gaps of the word-processed prose of your genealogy?). The retreat to small pasts at personal level will be exacerbated by the trend to larger political and economic frames of reference such as 'Europe' and 'the world' and the consequent diminishing of a sense of place in a nation state. Yet of course, counteracting that and again paradoxically, old nations like Britain will promote their individuality by appeals to their national heritage, of which one consequence will be the more forceful delineation within such nations of sub-group heritage such as that of the Scots, the Welsh, the Muslims and possibly even the English. It is curious that there is no *English* Folk Museum. Simultaneously, new nations will be busily creating their identifiable heritages, and so will the new supra-national groupings just as 'Europe' is trying to do now.

Domestically, much of the British heritage organisational structure could well change, even disintegrate, again within a complex of paradox. Large

161

organisations with the assets of momentum, professionalism and cost-efficiency will have to be sensitive to their members' needs and learn how to cope with them as mirrors of social change rather than distracting nuisances; they will also have to adapt so that they can continue to operate effectively at national level as the cutting edge of conservation shifts significantly to people-involvement at local level. 'I want to be involved in *my* heritage on my terms' is a cry which the national bodies will have to hear and accommodate. In parallel, of course, so will the locally-based organisations, many of which are already successfully doing exactly that. But satisfying and using volunteers is a continuous process, as anyone involved in voluntary work knows, and heritage-related activity has to compete with all the many other opportunities on offer to individuals for the fulfilling use of their time.

As in other fields too, the tensions of volunteers working in what is now a professional field have to be dissipated, something that conservation in general has successfully achieved but archaeology has not. Indeed, as the latter has undergone its very necessary phase of becoming professional during the last two decades, it has alienated many existing amateur archaeologists and driven interested parties into opposing groups. While there can be no going back on established and academic professional standards and functions, the now more widely recognised public role of archaeology with a social as well as a research function should during the 1990s contribute to a re-fusing of that traditional British strength, the alliance of professional and amateur. The probability is that, whether the former wants it or not, the latter will demand it, and especially in a sharing of access to the past.

Access is, of course, the general issue here. 'What sort of access to what sort of heritage?' is going to be one of the themes of the 1990s (Pl. 49). It will affect what is in museums, what they curate and what they collect, what they show and who is allowed to examine what is not on display. Some museums will close in the 1990s, perhaps mercifully; to whom will their collections belong? Who will decide, and on what criteria? Decisions about access will also affect who is allowed to visit what, when, out of doors. Will the National Trust be able to maintain its policy, justified in conservation terms, of closing country houses for six months of the year in the face of the growing pressure of the tourist industry to gain entry for its customers over a longer season? At what point is the paying visitor to the national heritage sites preserved on his behalf by the publicly-funded English Heritage going to jib at the ever-increasing entrance fee charged, on government instructions, by a commercially-oriented organisation and say 'But it's mine anyway – and I've already paid through my taxes'? Will foreign visitors come to be taxed for visiting 'our' heritage? Could Britain justify such a tax at, for example,

Stonehenge, where about three-quarters of the visitors are from abroad, visiting what is arguably as much their heritage as ours?

Then there is the small matter of the English landscape, currently exploited by British Rail self-hype as 'the greatest show on earth' – as viewed through the window of a train. That is the point: we are allowed to look at it, to enjoy visual access, but at least 90 per cent of it in Britain is the property of somebody else which denies us physical access. Of course, that is not absolutely true, for the countryside is criss-crossed by an amazing network of public rights of way, a controversial and legally-complex topic in its own right. The issues here, physical and philosophical, legal and practical, will certainly not lie down in the 1990s and, in a social context which generates strong emotions, even violence, it could well be that the proprietorial 'This is *my* land' point of view will have to cede ground to the more democratic 'This is *our* land' lobby (Pl. 50).

And what about the data-base underpinning the British heritage – who has access to that? Should you have to give a reason to an official for wanting to know what archaeological sites exist in your neighbourhood? Is it right for access to be determined by motive? Should you have to pay for that information, curated professionally maybe but often the result of altruistic endeavour? Is there any difference, for example, in buying a book of archaeological information, which we expect to pay for, and being charged for some one-off sheets of computer print-out with similar information? 'Whose past is it anyway?' quickly becomes 'Whose information about the past is it?' George Orwell saw this, remarking in one of his books that 'Who controls the past controls the future: who controls the present controls the past.' His shade may well ponder that as it looks at Wigan Pier now. The book was called *Ninety Eighty-Four*.

It is already six years since the calendrical 1984 when, it could be argued, nothing Orwellian happened; but posterity must be the judge of that and, with Isaiah Berlin, we must not dictate that judgement. Meanwhile, in many ways we cannot '. . . call back yesterday, bid time return'. A search for a time before is not nostalgia of that sort but rather an awareness of a fragile relationship, akin to that between us and our natural environment. That relationship is after all intellectual and cultural as much as physical. Our minds relate to a past, a series of pasts, call it what you will, which, thrusting on our gaze as physical survivals, nevertheless exists only through those minds. Maybe now, in the late twentieth century, we need to be as much stewards of that relationship as of the fabric of history itself.

We must be careful. The dead hands of our ancestors, in Richard Jeffries's phrase, could stretch forth from the tomb and drag us down just as easily as we ourselves could numb the past with conservation kindness. We must positively cultivate a past which, in Philip Larkin's words, is more than '. . . lighted rooms inside your head, and people in them acting'.

In the last resort, behind the façading, the fund-raising and the fun-making, 'then' is an intellectual construct honed by scholarship and research, 'now' and for each generation. If relational problem there be, as is probably becoming the case for present society, its creation and solution lie entirely with us and nowhere else. The past itself, unlike Nature, is inert; its present and future lie in our minds alone. Perhaps we should be asking not only 'Whose past?', but also 'Which pasts?' Paradoxically, and doubtless ambivalently, only the future will tell, for what has been will be.

42 Instant archaeology of the modern in the form of the earthworks of a deserted (1989) street within Peterlee New Town, County Durham (December). Cf. Pl. 45.

43 The north-west corner of the original, thirteenth-century city wall, Newcastle upon Tyne. The path and grass are recent, part of an enhancement scheme for the area. Beyond is the recently-restored House of Recovery, formerly an isolation hospital understandably just outside the walls, and now appropriately the headquarters of the North of England Museums Service, complete with conservation laboratory for 'sick' artefacts (December).

44 History happening amidst controversy and simultaneous commodification *en route* to becoming a (much-damaged) 'ancient' monument: the freshly-sprayed east face of the Berlin Wall (November).

45 Heritage ambivalence: can you come home to your heritage when it is not even built yet? On-site advertising board for an estate of new houses being constructed (December) by Heritage Homes at Peterlee New Town, County Durham. Cf. Pl. 42.

46 Past research consciously for the future: the experimental earthwork on Overton Down, Wiltshire, here seen twenty-eight years after its construction in 1960, with seventy-two years still to go to completion of its planned scientific life. It was designed purely to answer simple questions about what could have happened in prehistoric times to an artificial bank and ditch, e.g. how, why and over what period does the ditch fill up? What plants, in what sequence, colonise the bank? It has taken on an ancillary role as contemporary monitor during times of considerable land-use and environmental change, with considerable practical implications, and will undoubtedly be significant for unforeseen reasons in the twenty-first century.

47   Surrealist heritage: with St Columba and his coracle in the left background, a jolly cliché Viking warrior mannequin, complete with spurious horns on his helmet, stands along the Statue Walkway of eight historic figures ('Para Handy', 'Sunny Jim', etc.) in a labelled Heather Garden oblivious of a monorail caterpillar passing overhead. Part of the display by Argyll and the Isles Tourism Marketing Group, National Garden Festival, Gateshead.

48   One image of a past that never was, its subject one of perennial revelation and fantasy: the lively image inviting customers into the King Arthurs (no apostrophe) Arms, Tintagel, Cornwall.

168

9   Access to what? – here apparently to an undramatic circular ditch with an emotive name, King Arthur's Round Table, Yanwath, Cumbria. Mayburgh henge monument is in the background beneath the trees. These two archaeologically-important Properties-in-Care enjoy unimpeded public access, physically and visually, and are pregnant with significance to archaeologists who can 'read' them; but without on-site 'interpretation', they remain wrongly meaningful (nothing to do with King Arthur) or virtually meaningless to many who come to see them, and unknown to many potential visitors who could learn to appreciate them. 'Access' is a very complex and highly-charged issue.

0   Heritage can release strong emotions: scene outside the Aberconwy Centre, Llandudno, 2.19 p.m., 3 November, four minutes after an announcement from the chair that the hall had to be cleared because of a bomb threat just as the AGM of the National Trust was about to begin. The largest number of members ever to attend an AGM outside London had been about to debate two anti-hunting motions. Hunting as part of the British national and/or rural heritage is one of the arguments deployed in favour of its continuation.

169

Epilogue?

Forward to the past

And, in another New Year, the past continues. So does our dialogue with it. The above title is also that of a sitcom on television today, 1 January 1991.

The whole of the media are awash with pastness. Some of it was predictable, for at the end of any year they subject us to endless reviews of what has been. None of it is now; little of it is new. 'Chairman Ted rakes over the Ashes' has a certain tired familiarity about it as a headline; '1001 Nights of Television', far from being a futuristic horror fantasy is, thankfully but still unwatchably, 'archive night ... a three-hour trawl of TV history'. TV today contains silly history, 'A Connecticut Yankee in King Arthur's Court', and serious architectural history, 'English Towns: Richmond, North Yorkshire'; nostalgic heritage, 'Going Loco: the Final Puff', martial heritage with numerous programmes set in World War II, and fictional heritage with several 'period/costume dramas' ranging from *Little Dorrit* to an adventure set 'in an antique Cadillac'.

There's historic biography too: Cole Porter. Radio weighs in with 'A Vintage Breakfast' and 'some obscure places where Latin still flourishes' before most of the population is awake, climaxing at peak time with forty-five minutes of commemorative navel-gazing, a 'critical look' at 'The First 40 Years' of 'The Archers'. Does that count as historical fiction, fictional history or a history of a fiction? In contrapuntal distinction, its contents by definition otherwise virtually all 'musical heritage' laced today with various traditional and commemorative programmes, Radio 3 devotes all of fifteen minutes to an item continuing the 'encapsulated history of mankind'. Who says we haven't got our priorities right?

A selection from a quick scan of but three daily papers (*G*, *DM* and *J*) for this first day of 1991 reveals a similar dialogue with all sorts of pasts and their manifestations. Obviously *they* believe there is an interest in old things and times before out there; it is that they print this sort of

Epilogue?

material at all, rather than what they report or whether they do so correctly, which says so much about us.

Reported today, for example, is the annual foray into the Public Records Office where hitherto confined documents are released under the thirty-year rule. As usual, what proved of significance in journalistic terms is mainly the revelation of the non-availability of various 'sensitive' items from 1960 and indeed earlier. 'The decision to withhold the 1940 documents [about Gibraltar] demonstrates the extent of sensitivity in Whitehall about the relationship of past events ... to contemporary problems.' Not only in Whitehall, one might add. Thank you, Richard Norton-Taylor, for a pithy statement of the sub-text to this book.

Among records *actually* made available is evidence from 1960 of Britain's concern about its ability to repulse an Iraqi attack on Kuwait, a British Protectorate since 1899 but then soon to become independent. Six thousand British troops were airlifted to Kuwait in 1961, a fairly major and successful operation completely unremarked, as far as I am aware, in current nostalgic jingoism rejoicing in the return of the 'Desert Rats', 1940s vintage, to foreign sands. But in the contest among the images of the past for our contemporary attention, Kuwait thirty years ago is a non-starter, even though it could be about to start a major war. Nearly half the population was not even born then! So how can an anonymous, isolated and bloodless episode compete with the many visual replayings in cinema and on TV over their lifetimes of an epic, fast-moving struggle in alien surroundings between identifiably 'good' and 'bad' forces led from the front by charismatic and articulate heroes with tanks? Kuwait 1961 is nevertheless more relevant to matters which may well engulf the world in war a fortnight from now than the North Africa of 'Monty' and Rommel.

The contemporary 'green' influence on history is witnessed in the news item that the Department of the Environment has become 'the most unpopular ministry in Whitehall history'.

Lord Chorley of Kendal, 'who slips into the hot seat today as chairman of the politically riven National Trust, ... has a deep sense of history ... some decisions ... during his chairmanship may well be criticised as anti-democratic ... There are members who feel that the trust, with its huge holdings of land and historic homes, has come to see itself more as an impersonal museum curator than as a preserver of a rural way of life ... he faces a term as chairman in which controversy will be unavoidable.'

How accurately that piece reflects basic issues: what sort of Trust? Access, but how and to what sort of heritage? Does the Trust have a social role (as its founders clearly intended) and, if so, how can it, indeed should it, reconcile preserving archaic ways of life while meeting the needs of contemporary life-styles? Focused on the Trust, for better or for worse, these and similar fundamentals will continue to beg questions of and about heritage and society and its numerous organisations throughout the 1990s.

'... she is a legend'; 'She is truly a legend.' Of 'La Stupenda' at her farewell performance, so-dubbed 'when she conquered La Scala 30 years ago', otherwise Joan Sutherland, not Margaret Thatcher.

'The original Tower of London may have been a Roman lighthouse ... A light on top of a long-demolished section of octagonal tower, within the walls of the top tourist attraction (Oh! anachronism most wonderful!), would have marked the point at which ships tied up to pay river dues charged in Anglo-Saxon times ... The missing tower ... is marked on maps published in 1681 and 1774. It burned down in the 1770s. Beefeater tradition has it that the Tower used to boast a navigational light ...'

The piece can safely be awarded now the 1991 prize for the shortest archaeo-historical news item with the mostest. It has the lot: a major site, mystery, a plausible chain of varied evidence from a Roman tile to Beefeater tradition, tourist interest, and the chance of being a scoop if correct. But in any case it is a splendid story, typical of *The Daily Mail* and of the populist past as presented for tit-bit consumption. To be fair to *The Daily Mail*, this number contains very little other pastness.

My local paper prints a 'Special' to mark the 76th running of the Morpeth–Newcastle New Year's Day race, 'Britain's oldest and most traditional road race' (later: rather unfairly again won by a southerner as it happens, but a Morpeth lad won it in 1974).

Apprehension blossoms at the prospect discussed in a feature article of major changes to the Victorian Park outside my window – 'my' Park, 'my heritage', daily enjoyed almost because of its air of faded nobility of intent and actual semi-dereliction. Apparently, however, it 'is currently the subject of an international design competition aimed at revamping it – with the inclusion of an ambitious underwater world tourist attraction'. Now, it's all very well writing and lecturing about such things as an interesting phenomenon but, without in any way wishing to be accused of nimbyism, to have proposals of that sort about one's own environs under serious consideration *by others* is a bit much, as I am sure you would agree.

'Work is expected to start early in the new year on the excavation

Epilogue?

of ...' – Stonehenge? The Tower of London? The Palace of the Roman Emperor at York? A fabulous treasure-grave of a Dark Age King? Well, er, no ... – '... Britain's forgotten underground air force.' Flying moles? Projectile worms? Space-ship tube-trains? Not at all: 'At least 23 dismantled wartime planes ... have been located by the Bomber Airfield Society. "We are confident we know the exact whereabouts of the planes – enough to form an air force of our own," said Dr Keith Percival-Barker, the society's secretary' (he had better be careful what he says – they might be needed) '... The society's main find ... is thought to be half a squadron of Lancasters ... [It] is converting part of the former RAF Binbrook station, near Grimsby, to show any restored aircraft it recovers ... "so that people can climb inside and feel what it was like".'

Clearly, of the past there is no end, nor of its heritagisation. Still, just think of the possibility at the centenary of the Battle of Britain (2040) of not just a solitary Lancaster, but a *whole squadron of them*, flying past and bringing Heathrow to a halt for hours, not minutes. Such potential of the past in the future should be given serious thought – now.

But meanwhile, stop the past; I want to get off ...

Bibliographical note

My material has been culled from acquaintance with several thousand information leaflets and other ephemera, newspapers and magazines, and radio and television. Much of it is therefore unreferenceable in the normal academic way, though sources are given, or at least indicated, as far as possible.

Nevertheless, no book can exist in intellectual isolation and the purpose of this note is to indicate other books and publications which, while they may not have been used directly as sources, treat aspects touched on in this book. Often, of course, they do so with greater authority and in greater detail than here, so another purpose of this note is to indicate some 'Further Reading'.

General

My immediate precursors, each with a different viewpoint, are clearly David Lowenthal, *The Past is a Foreign Country* (1985), Patrick Wright, *On Living in an Old Country* (1986) and Robert Hewison, *The Heritage Industry* (1987). Lowenthal is the most scholarly, his book a landmark. Wright's is the most dense, even though it was written as a reaction to a contemporary situation; Hewison, writing a percipient polemic as a spin-off to his series of literary and cultural histories, probably had the most immediate effect and yet curiously already has the air of a period piece.

The underlying issues here have of course exercised academics and cultural commentators for some time. Collingwood's *The Idea of History*

(1946), and Butterfield's *History and Human Relations* (1951), for example, remain pertinent, and a range of more recent 'nature of history-type' books would include J. H. Plumb's *The Death of the Past* (1969) and M. I. Finley's *The Use and Abuse of History* (1985) (with an excellent bibliography). Symposia-type books range from the still useful H. P. R. Finberg (ed.) *Approaches to History* (1962) to J. Gardiner (ed.) *The History Debate* (1990). Barbara Tuchman's *Practicing History* (1981) provides a one-person, transatlantic symposium of which Lewis Binford's *In Pursuit of the Past* is a near-contemporary, anthropological equivalent. The older *Archaeology and Society* (1939, 3rd edn 1960) by Grahame Clark has the merits of both a period piece and a pioneering essay, still full of wise and relevant observations. For a contemporary but different philosophical point of view, questioning many of the assumptions in most of the above, and here, try, for example, Karl Popper's *The Poverty of Historicism* (1957 and, most pertinently, still in print).

More recently, archaeological theory about itself and what it is supposed, or what it thinks it is supposed, to be doing has become simultaneously convoluted and fragmented: of Ian Hodder's several books *Reading the Past* (1986) has the merit of being short in arguing an archaeology-is-history position but other writers tend to take up much more time and space in occupying various positions in such fields as material culture, palaeo-socio-economics and feminism. Shanks and Tilley's two 1987 books provide food for thought and references: *Social Theory and Archaeology* and

Bibliographical note

Re-constructing Archaeology: Theory and practice. Thoughtful considerations of matters central to this book, especially the papers by Cleere and Lewthwaite, are contained in *Extracting Meaning from the Past* edited by John Bintliff (1988). Peter Ackroyd imposes various meanings in his archaeologically well-informed novel *First Light* (1989), an intriguing version of prehistory in the present which should perhaps be listed under Chapter 8. Penelope Lively's *Treasures of Time* (1979) is one of the very few other successful novels in this difficult field. The CBA's *British Archaeology: An introductory booklist* (1987) fulfils its intended purpose, so much of the following, in naming archaeological books, picks out publications subsequent to it.

Of general applicability throughout this book is also *The Cambridge Illustrated Dictionary of British Heritage* (ed. A. Isaacs and J. Monk, 1987), HRH the Prince of Wales's *A Vision of Britain: A personal view of architecture* (1989), and David Cannadine's *The Pleasures of the Past* (1990).

Contemporaneity in past matters is provided in numerous annual reports, bulletins, magazines and journals. Those of EH, NT and the English Royal Commission are always interesting, particularly when the interest is for reasons other than intended; similar publications pour from other relevant bodies like the Countryside Commission and the Nature Conservancy Council, the National Parks and numerous local authorities. Equally, no voluntary conservation body counts for anything unless it too is publishing likewise, both for its members and in the taking of public stances; so there is an extensive alternative literature too. The Civic Trust's *Environmental Directory* (1988 and periodically updated) provides the *entrée* to the organisations at national level. The absolutely essential annual for the facts and figures of contemporaneous use of the past is the English Tourist Board's *English Heritage Monitor*.

Among periodicals, *Antiquity* is also essential, not least for its editorials; *British Archaeological News* (CBA) is always up to date and authoritative, which is more than can be said for the otherwise useful *Popular Archaeology* (which has not been used at all in writing this book). Political bias is also apparent in *Heritage* (Bulldog Magazines Ltd) but for the real centre of Establishment heritage and its attitudes look at *Country Life, The Field* and, for fine art, *The Burlington Magazine*. Soft-focus edges to heritagism are apparent in such as *The World of Interiors. History Today* speaks for itself.

Past introductions: Chapters 1–2

Joseph Campbell's *The Hero with a Thousand Faces* (1988), and the 1990 TV series based on his work, obviously inspired my opening; so did the Bible, a major heritage work: see *Archaeology and the Bible* (1990) by Tubb and Chapman and, more generally, David Wilson's (ed.) *The Collections of the British Museum* and *The British Museum, Purpose and politics* (1989; all British Museum Publications). Ellis Davidson's *Gods and Myths of Northern Europe* (1964, currently in print, Penguin) surveys more local Campbell country. Colin Renfrew's Cambridge inaugural lecture, *Towards an Archaeology of Mind* (1982) inspired one line of thought in mine. His *Archaeology, Theories, Methods and Practice* (1991), with Paul Bahn, comprehensively oversees the whole scene and is bibliographically well-endowed.

Sidling up to heritage from many directions is a great range of books, varying from the magisterial works of a century ago by Ruskin and Morris, through what might be identified as the 1930s 'Batsford heritage syndrome' represented by books such as *England's Heritage* (1935), *The British Heritage* (1948, Odhams) and Clough Williams-Ellis's (ed.) *Britain and the Beast* (1937, Dent), to the Department of the Environment's *What is our Heritage?* (1975) and the independent sector's *Rescue Archaeology* (1974, ed. P. Rahtz). A 1980s strain of more rigorous intellectuality is symbolised historically by Charles Dellheim's *The Face of the Past: The preservation of the medieval inheritance in Victorian England* (1982) and P. Levine, *The Amateur and the Professional: antiquarians, historians and archaeologists in Victorian England 1838–1886* (1985); and, agonisingly, by Lowenthal and Binney's (eds) *Our Past before Us: Why do we save it?* (1981). They and others lead up to four volumes orig-

nating in the first World Archaeological Congress 1986: Shennan (ed.) *Archaeological
Approaches to Cultural Identity* (1989),
Gathercole and Lowenthal (eds) *The Politics of
the Past* (1989), and, both Layton (ed.), *Who
needs the Past? Indigenous values and archaeology* (1988) and *Conflict in the Archaeology of
Living Traditions* (1988). See also J. Greenfield,
The Return of Cultural Treasures (1989), and
'. Baker and J. Thomas (eds), *Writing the Past
n the Present* (1990).

A geographical interest in all this is represented
by, for example, Jay Appleton's studies,
especially *The Experience of Landscape* (1986)
and Cosgrove and Daniels's (eds) *The Icon-
ography of Landscape* (1988), both discussing
approaches through perceptions stimulating
especially to those who have 'seen' landscape
only historically and archaeologically. There is
of course a vast landscape literature emanating
from geography which ought to be more influential in archaeological thinking than is the case
(and *vice versa*). The Penguin Guide to the
Landscape of England and Wales (ed. P.
Coones and J. Patten, 1986) is an easily accessible *entrée* though it is not perfect and has
no bibliography. Return to the C. C. Taylor
annotation (1985) of Hoskins's classic *The
Making of the English Landscape* or use his
Village and Farmstead (1983). J. Wagstaff (ed.)
Landscape and Culture (1987) tries to link
geography and archaeology and contains quite a
lot that is useful.

On more specific aspects in these chapters, T.
Darvill, *Prehistoric Britain* (1987) is the most
reliable of the modern British prehistories, with
M. Jones's *England before Domesday* (1986)
providing an environmental slant and coming
nearer to the present. Of the many guides to
archaeological sites, J. Dyer's Penguin on *Prehistoric England and Wales* (1981), C. Houl-
der's *Wales: An Archaeological Guide* (Faber,
974), and the Scottish Royal Commission's
eight paperbacks in its *Exploring Scotland's
Heritage* series are the best; otherwise, given
the many deficient publications, sound advice
is to buy a local book when you get there. Most
of the 'official' sites have their own guidebooks.
Lord Montagu introduced a collection of low-
level, oblique balloon views of *English Heritage
from the Air* by Neil Burton; Magnus Magnus-
son edited in *Echoes in Stone* (1983) a similar

introduction to sites cared for by the Ancient
Monuments Board for Scotland. Muir and
Welfare produced *The National Trust Guide
to Prehistoric and Roman Britain* (1983) which
is not confined to NT properties; Fowler and
Sharp's *Images of Prehistory* (1990) is not a
guide but it illustrates a representative selection
of British sites, bringing out their contexts and
architectural and landscape qualities. In
general, the many Shire books, on periods,
themes and types of site, are reliable and useful
introductions.

This author's *The Farming of Prehistoric
Britain* (1983) discusses exactly that but it has
been overtaken by new research and should
be read in conjunction with R. Mercer's (ed.)
Farming Practice in British Prehistory (1981).
A. Fleming's *The Dartmoor Reaves* (1989) will
be a revelation to those who think they know
their English landscape and its agriculture.
Similarly, the Coles' *Sweet Track to Gla-
stonbury* (1986) reveals a whole aspect of the
buried past and a chapter of remarkable English
landscape archaeology; ditto Charles Thomas's
Exploration of a Drowned Landscape (1985)
for one we have lost and rediscovered. Oliver
Rackham's *History of the Countryside* (1986)
is authoritative but not a history; the *History
of the English Landscape* series tends to be the
reverse. Martin Carver interprets urban archaeology in *Underneath English Towns* (1987) and
John Percival's *Living in the Past* (1980) tells
the story of the BBC 'Iron Age' experience.

Pasts with people: Chapters 3–6

Museums and museology have their own considerable literature, not least the monthly
Museums Journal. For present purposes Robert
Lumley's (ed.) *The Museum Time-Machine*
(1988) is relevant, its topics apposite and its
footnotes providing an entry into the published
background. Simon Tait's journalistic journey
to *Palaces of Discovery: The changing world
of Britain's museums* (1989) produces a well-
informed, unauthorised survey, coun-
terpointing much 'official' and professional
literature such as John Thompson's (ed.)
Manual of Curatorship (1984) and the 1990
New Visions for Independent Museums by V.
T. Middleton. Kenneth Hudson's *Museums of
Influence* (1987) provides a global context in a
judgemental survey.

Bibliographical note

Among a whole library of books about the countryside and present concerns, numerous publications by the Council for the Protection of Rural England are noteworthy; its *Rural England: Our countryside at the crossroads* (1988) gives a well-informed and revealing flavour. Two Open University/Countryside Commission books, both originally 1985, are also well informed and less romantically inclined: *The Changing Countryside* and *The Countryside Handbook* are basic for students. Another two books, both by Howard Newby, provide an historical and sociological framework: *Green and Pleasant Land? Social change in rural England* (1979) and *Country Life: A social history of rural England* (1987).

G.E. Mingay's two-volume (1981) *The Victorian Countryside* provides the sort of academic rigour so often lacking in public presentation of rustic heritage and is indicative of much other historical research into nineteenth-century and earlier countrysides. Richard Morris's *Churches in the Landscape* (1989) provides an eye-opening approach to one of the most-visited and characteristic buildings in the countryside; Richard and Nina Muir perceptively discuss a phenomenon taken even more for granted in *Fields* (1989). What others have previously thought and seen is exemplified in Denys Thompson's anthology *Change and Tradition in Rural England* (1980); Ronald Blythe could be in such a work in future but meanwhile enjoy, for example, his *Characters and their Landscapes* (1982) or, better still, read any of George Ewart Evans's books. Living with all sorts of pasts is quite amusingly commented on anthropologically by Nigel Barley in *Native Land: The bizarre rituals and curious customs that make the English English* (1989).

Many bodies such as SAVE and the Society for the Protection of Ancient Buildings continue to express concern about what is happening to and in the countryside. An example of the sort of publication available is English Heritage, *The Conversion of Historic Farm Buildings* (n.d. but 1990).

Among all this learning and concern it is a pleasure to acknowledge a very thin book motivated by, and intended to serve nothing but, interest: Watlington Parish History Group, *Watlington: Pictures from the past* (n.d. b 1990).

Past workings: Chapters 7–11

Far and away the most revealing source abo present heritage management in England ar Wales is the *First Report* of the House Commons Environment Committee called *H toric Buildings and Ancient Monuments* vols, 1987). This is essential for any attempt understand not only what is going on but als what those in the business *think* is going on.

On the wider scene, *Ethics and Values Archaeology* (1984) edited by E.L. Green pr vides a transatlantic case study of some of t deeper issues lying behind the management the past, initially aired in McGimsey's *Publ Archaeology* (1972). Schiffer and Gun merman's *Conservation Archaeology: A gui for cultural resource management studi* (1977) includes a lot of the principle still bas to present practice and an exhaustive bi liography to North American developmen before its publication. Its lead was followed b Cleere's (ed.) *Approaches to the Archaeologic Heritage* (1984), brought up to date an extended in the same editor's indispensab *Archaeological Heritage Management in t Modern World* (1989). Training for this field international level is discussed in a forthcomin volume (originating in the Second Wor Archaeological Congress 1990) edited by Clee and Fowler (Routledge, forthcoming).

R.M. Newcomb's *Planning the Past* (197 remains helpful but is inevitably becomin dated, as is David Baker's *Living with the Pas The historic environment* (1983). The latt remains, however, the best discussion of th English situation, being particularly strong its explanation of the local authority rol *Welsh Archaeological Heritage*, edited by I Moore and D. Austin (1986), does likewise fo the principality. Many county councils hav now produced 'heritage' documents of one so or another: Hampshire's *Hampshire's Heritag and a Policy for its Future* (1979) was and is published model which few have equalled. Th present position is selectively reviewed in M Whewell, 'The Historic Environment in th Hands of Local Government' (MA dissertatio

University of Newcastle upon Tyne, 1990). Wider issues are addressed in relation to a particularly 1980s phenomenon in P. M. J. Boniface, 'Heritage in Post-Industrial Urban Areas of England; with particular reference to Tyneside, Merseyside and London Docklands' (MA dissertation, University of Newcastle upon Tyne, 1989).

DoE, *Environmental Assessment: A guide to the procedures* (1989) is an essential manual for advisers and practitioners; similarly MAFF's *Environmentally Sensitive Areas* (1989) explains the concept and the practice. Perhaps surprisingly, the same Ministry is also responsible for the extraordinarily useful *Historic Farm Buildings Study: Sources of Information* (1985), compiled by Nigel Harvey.

The Museums and Galleries Commission has provided a factual survey of *The National Museums: The national museums and galleries of the United Kingdom* (1988). *Treasures for the Nation: Conserving our heritage* (1988, British Museum Publications for the National Heritage Memorial Fund), catalogued the Fund's purchases which were on exhibition, thereby neatly defining 'national heritage' in practice, and included among several interesting articles 'The National Heritage: The development of an idea since 1870' by John Cornforth. Arthur Jones's *Britain's Heritage. The Creation of the National Heritage Memorial Fund* (1985) is another useful account. Also at the national level, the Countryside Commission is a great publisher of its own works, many of them free, e.g. *Countryside Commission News*, a magazine *inter alia* listing current publications. A survey of *Britain's National Parks* was edited by W. S. Lacey (1984) updated in John Wyatt's *A Visitor's Guide to the National Parks of England and Wales* (1988). George Lambrick edited *Archaeology and Nature Conservation* (1985), still the best discussion of this aspect in print.

In *Recording Historic Buildings: A descriptive specification* (1990) the Royal Commission on the Historical Monuments of England defines standards to meet one need and exemplifies professional standards now required for data-enhancement in heritage management. The urgency is illustrated by the same Commission's *Architectural Survey of Urban Development Corporation Areas: Tyne and Wear. Volume 1: Tyneside* (1990). Similar motives activated the immaculate publication of *North-East Perth: An archaeological landscape* (1990) from the Scottish Royal Commission.

The role of English Heritage is amply documented in its numerous publications, especially its *Annual Report* and its annual *Archaeology Review* which explains in detail how and why it spends *c*. £10 million a year on archaeology overall including, currently, £5.6 million a year on rescue archaeology. Also particularly useful are its *Conservation Bulletin* and, from its education branch, *Remnants*. It broke new ground with its admirable *Ancient Monuments in the Countryside: An archaeological management review* (1987) by T. Darvill, who also wrote *The Archaeology of the Uplands* (1986) for RCHME and the CBA. Another selected block of heritage, *The Conservation Areas of England* (1990) is surveyed by Graham Pearce and others.

M. R. Apted *et al.*, *Ancient Monuments and their Interpretation* (1977) explores the traditional official approach to nearly a hundred years of monumental guardianship, further clarified by M. W. Thompson in *Ruins: Their preservation and display* (1981). Different views are discussed in *The Management and Presentation of Field Monuments* (1986) edited by Hughes and Rowley. Best practice on excavations and projects is spelt out in English Heritage's *Visitors Welcome* (1988). Exemplary items in a lively literature about heritage interpretation are the *Proceedings of the First World Congress on Heritage Presentation and Interpretation* (1988), edited by John Lunn, and (from the Second such Congress) *Heritage Interpretation* (2 vols, 1989), edited by David Uzzell.

Some of the background to the practicalities mentioned in Chapter 8 are discussed in Chippendale *et al.*, *Who Owns Stonehenge?* (1990), itself a sequel in some respects to the same author's *Stonehenge Complete* (1983). Archaeological information about the area has now been transformed by J. Richards, *The Stonehenge Environs Project* (1990). The other half of this World Heritage Site now has a magnificent addition to its literature, *Avebury*

Bibliographical note

Reconsidered: From the 1660s to the 1990s (1991) by P. J. Ucko *et al*. The best academic book on the Wall is Breeze and Dobson, *Hadrian's Wall* (1987), supplemented now by Stephen Johnson's illustrated guide book of the same title (1989). Some of my remarks are based on the Countryside Commission's *The Hadrian's Wall Path: Proposed national trail from Wallsend to Bowness-on-Solway. Informal consultation* (1990).

There are several books about the history of the National Trust and the development of its particular proprietorial management: see for example, Robin Fedden's *The Continuing Purpose* (1968) and John Gaze, *Figures in a Landscape* (1988). Just what 'history' can be present in any area, and how perceptions of it can change with research, are pleasingly narrated by Richard Hodges in his punningly-titled *Wall-to-Wall History: The story of Roystone Grange* (1991), an area in the Peak National Park. Much debate about commons in the late 1980s, including the *Report* of the Common Lands Forum, tended to stress the significance, at least implicitly, of the basic *Commons and Village Greens: A study in land use, conservation and management based on a national survey . . .* (1967) by Denham, Roberts and Smith. R. A. Buchanan's *Industrial Archaeology in Britain* (1980) is the authority for a field touched on in several places but not developed in my discussion; Keith Falconer's *Guide to England's Industrial Heritage* (1980) is the authoritative *vade mecum*. Vernacular architecture, another major component of the British heritage, can be approached through the works of Maurice Barley, e.g. *Houses and History* (Faber, 1986), and R. W. Brunskill, e.g. *Traditional Buildings of Britain: An introduction to vernacular architecture* (1982). Similarly D. R. Wilson, *Air Photo Interpretation for Archaeologists* (1982) can serve as a readily available entry to another field lightly touched on here. RCHME's *The Emerging Past: Air photography and the buried landscape* (1989) literally reveals the complex.

J. Mackay, *Collecting Local History* (1984) has a good bibliography, some of which is quoted. Philip Riden's *Local History* (1983) is a good handbook for beginners.

Tourism of course has a huge literature of its own now, some of it academic, some commercial. Douglas Pearce, *Tourism Today: A geographical analysis* (1987) is a useful entry point, with a long bibliography, and a good example of one academic approach. I. Ousby, *The Englishman's England: Taste, travel and the rise of tourism* (1990), provides a modern historical study of a phenomenon with its roots in the writings of Defoe and Fiennes: see Esther Moir, *The Discovery of Britain: The English tourists 1540–1840* (1964).

The *Guide to English Heritage Properties* and the National Trust *Handbook* for members and visitors are published annually. Otherwise just visit your Tourist Information Centre and collect the freebies, such as those freely quoted here, or buy for under £5 one of the professional and/or commercial guidebooks to a theme, such as country houses, or an area. Shire, for example, publishes an excellent series of cheap pocket-size county guides.

Basically, newspapers and magazines, and especially their advertisements, street hoardings and auction room catalogues provide background to Chapter 11. Sotheby's *Guide Antiques and their prices worldwide*, annually is revealing, of mentality as much as price. Council of Europe, *Metal Detectors and Archaeology* (Doc. 4741–E, Strasbourg, 1981) illustrates the international dimension of on not unrelated practical problem. More generally, K. Meyer's *The Plundered Past* (1973) is still unfortunately only too germane. My particular grouse is Ordnance Survey, *Historical Map and Guide: Hadrian's Wall* (1989).

Though not in appropriate company here, P. J. Reynolds, *Iron Age Farm: The Butser experiment* (1979) discusses scientific research in the context of a public show-piece site.

Past projections: Chapter 12

A Usable Past: Essays in European cultural history (1990) by W. J. Bouwsma is my starting point and reference quarry. Philip Norman's *The Age of Parody* (1990), especially its eponymous first essay, was much in mind. So too, among a far-too-fast growing post-modernist literature, was David Kolb's *Postmodern Sophistications: Philosophy, architecture and tradition* (1990) and Robert Hewison's *Future*

Tense: A new art for the nineties (1990). In the background were the vibes of continuing debates on the 'heritage industry', as signalled, for example, in *The Dodo Strikes Back* (1988) and 'Archaeology and the Heritage Industry' (*Archaeological Review from Cambridge* 7:2, 1988); and about nostalgia itself as exemplified in Shaw and Chase (eds), *The Imagined Past: History and nostalgia* (1989), complementing F. Davis's earlier *Yearning for Yesterday: A sociology of nostalgia* (1979). Personally, I think George Orwell said or implied most of it earlier still in *Nineteen Eighty-Four* (1949), a comment which makes inevitable a reference to R. Williams, *Culture and Society: Coleridge to Orwell* (1987).

'Green' literature is now voluminous: let Jonathon Porritt and David Winner, *The Coming of the Greens* (1988) suffice as entry to it, reminding ourselves of its historical dimension, studied so perceptively by Keith Thomas in *Man and the Natural World: Changing attitudes in England 1500–1800* (1983). Modern scientific views of earlier relationships are presented in Simmons and Tooley, *The Environment in British Prehistory* (1981), now superseded at the global scale by the former's *Changing the Face of the Earth: Culture, environment, history* (1989).

One sort of access is predicted by the English Tourist Board, *Visitors in the Countryside:*

Rural tourism. A development strategy (1988) and one sort of official provision is described and assessed in John Blunden and Nigel Curry, *A People's Charter? Forty Years of the National Parks and Access to the Countryside Act* (HMSO, 1990). Marion Shoard inveighs against the denial of access in *The Theft of the Countryside* (1980) and *This Land is our Land* (1987), a theme discussed in Williamson and Bellamy's *Property and Landscape: A social history of land ownership and the English countryside* (1987) and illustrated photographically by Fay Godwin in *Our Forbidden Land* (1990). An alternative view is displayed, for example, in *The Field* and any Saturday in *The Weekend Telegraph.*

Three other special interests are mentioned: Paul Devereux in *Places of Power: Secret energies at ancient sites: A guide to observed or measured phenomena* (1990) argues the case for quite widely-held beliefs; and Linda Anderson, editor of *Plotting Change: Contemporary women's fiction* (1990), can stand symbol for a highly sensitive issue of significance in more than a mere heritage context with her article 'The Re-Imagining of History in Contemporary Women's Fiction'. It somehow seems appropriate to end with a book subtitled 'Archaeology in Education'. Edited by P. Stone and R. Mackenzie, it is called *The Excluded Past* (1990).

Index

Index

Index

Index

Index

Index